Cattitude Is Everything

6 Lessons from Cats to Live Your
Best Life

Brian Basterfield

Contents

A Free Gift to The Readers

Thank you for choosing to read this book. I hope you find it insightful and practical.

To enhance your experience and provide additional value, I've included the following material at no extra cost to you:

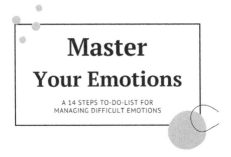

Master Your Emotions

A 14 STEPS TO-DO-LIST FOR MANAGING DIFFICULT EMOTIONS

This supplementary content offers valuable insights related to managing your emotions.

To access your bonus material, please scan the QR code below:

Thank you for your support, and enjoy your reading!

Introduction

Have you ever been sitting with your cat in your lap, stressing about day-to-day life? There are bills to pay, work deadlines to meet, and you have no idea what you are going to do about dinner. Do you think that your cat has any of those worries floating around in his head? Of course not; he looks so calm, preening himself, giving a gentle purr every now and then, safe in the knowledge that he is the boss of the house.

When he looks at you, and your heart melts, you wonder what his furry little brain is telling him. Behind his dark green eyes, there is a wise 'catty-mind.' Ah, if only he could talk. What would he say? He'd probably be smart enough to identify your childhood traumas and to playfully tease you about that time you knocked your shin and swore at the coffee table as if it wasn't your fault.

He looks a little smug, but he's a cat; that's his vibe. Nothing phases him, and he chuckles to himself, knowing he is on top of the world as he sits satisfied on your lap. You think to yourself, 'What a handsome little scoundrel. He'd probably be a psychologist if he could talk.' Then you say out loud, 'That would save me some bucks!' He looks up at you, and his face tells you that he is hungry–you grin slightly, knowing that you have your priorities straight–John Garfield III, as you named your furry feline friend, will always be fed first.

You prepare Johnny G's food, and as you watch him eat it, you wonder why he has not written a book yet. While licking his lips, he looks up at you, and you swear you hear him say, 'hooman, if I wrote a book, I would become too famous, and then I would have to share you.' You can't help but smile as Jonny G stretches, walks to the kitchen door, and turns his head as if to say, 'Are you coming to pet me or no?' You say out loud, 'It's clear who rules the roost, well not quite roost, but you know what I mean John-John.'

If only humans could communicate as well, and with such ease, as you readers and your collective cats do. All the John Garfield III's out there have so much to teach us, mere mortals. In this book, I will harness all the positive cat power in the world while I take you through a transition. With the right 'cattitude' and the inspiration that comes from our fearless, feline friends, you will learn the approach to living your best life.

It all begins with communication, and yes, my friends, this is a skill that we practice effortlessly with our cats. Well, to be fair, our cats may be looking at us and thinking, 'Wow, these humans are dumb...lovable...but dumb.' Okay, I guess that doesn't get us very far on the communication road, but the point is that effective communication is not practiced enough. In all types of relationships, be they personal, professional, romantic, or otherwise, some form of communication is required.

Part of me wants to say that communication to a human is like lasagna to a cat. The more, the better! I was going to say less is more, but give John Garfield III or Jim Davis' Garfield a lasagna, and they will always want more. Right, so it is settled. The more communication, the better.

Let me assure you that you are in good hands. My background in organizational management and my passion for helping people to reach their communication goals are some of the tools that I have relied on to write this book. I have always been interested in psychology and the human condition, as well as the notion that we can achieve more if we can laugh at ourselves. We all know that our cats internally laugh at us...yes, I said at us–sometimes with, but mostly at.

I know how difficult communication *can* be. Just ask my brain when it tells my fingers what strings to hold down on my guitar but gets completely ignored.

The contents of this book are anecdotal and practical, with theoretical elements where necessary. Communication does go further than just a discussion–my time in leadership positions, which required problem-solving and strategic planning skills, taught me that. Luckily for you, the cat-loving readers, I will impart those lessons with passion and care.

If you feel like you are in a rut, unfulfilled, and in need of a change–a positive one–I will assist you in making the change. Perhaps you are struggling with confidence or self-doubt, and you don't have the words to communicate these issues. I will give you those words...never again will you hear, 'cat got your tongue?'

I am hoping to take you out of your comfort zone but also to show you the importance of self-care and relaxation. There is always much to be learned about ourselves, and doing so can empower us with confidence and purpose. Every reader is unique, just like their cats, and as we know, uniqueness makes us beautiful...just like our...you guessed it, our cats. I want you to embrace who you are as a person, take inspiration from your preening partners in crime, and allow me to help you find the love, gratitude, and joy that you deserve.

Talking of being unique, we will start with lessons on how to embrace your unique 'purrsonality.' Next up is possibly the best cue we can take from our catnap masters—the art of relaxation. Mindful meditation is a large component of relaxation, and there are some wonderful tips waiting for you. You will receive an injection of curiosity—I know what you're thinking—but finding adventure brought the curious cat back to life. Through the help of our four-legged fur balls, I will assist you in injecting adventure into your life.

If cats could speak, we know without a doubt that they would speak their minds. As humans, it can be difficult to do so, but don't panic. As you progress through this book, your 'mind-speaking' skills will be honed. Have you ever seen a cat doubting itself? Never! You will soon become like the self-assured cat, fiercely independent and able to thrive as your own person.

So, feed your figurative John Garfield III, put your feet up, and get ready to take a cat-fueled journey with me as I show you how to become the master of your best life. I am willing to bet, though, that when your cat hops up onto your lap and places their head against your book, they will be thinking, 'Oh were you reading this? It's just that I am desperate for a nap right here and right now.' That's okay. Just gently shift positions so you are both comfortable and you can see the pages clearly...here we go.

Chapter 1

Embrace Your Inner Purrsonality

Discovering Your Unique Traits and Talents

I ndividuality is important, and we often have the notion that we don't fit in because we are different...do you think a cat cares if he or she doesn't fit in? The idiosyncrasies and quirks of our cats make them unique, and there is beauty in uniqueness. So, let's jump right in and embrace our human traits and talents.

Getting Personal

Although society prefers conformity, that doesn't mean that society is correct, and it also doesn't mean that we *have to* conform. The ways to embrace your uniqueness can be split up into 13 categories. Because we are all different, the entirety of the content in each category won't always apply, but let's just say that you have 13 potential lives–nine more than your cat!

Remind Yourself How Important It Is To Be Unique

You can give yourself pep talks if you start feeling negative about your uniqueness, starting by telling yourself that there is nothing negative about it. Uniqueness is valuable because it is rare (cue the conformity part). If you are authentic, you don't have to hide anything, and that fact is tied to happiness. Plus, others will draw inspiration and confidence from you.

Accept Diversity

If you are not willing to accept other people for their uniqueness, then you can't expect to be accepted for *your* uniqueness. Imagine if we all looked the same–that would suck! If we all look different, then we can all have different hobbies, varying tastes in music, alternative ways of carrying ourselves, and, well, the confidence to accept diversity in ourselves and in others. Live your life in a way that you apply your abilities to your interests without fear of judgment, and you will feel empowered and liberated.

It's Your Story

A dog may listen to you, but if your cat could talk and you gave an instruction, you could expect a 'whatever' and an eye roll...that little furry rascal lives by its own story...you need to do the same. If you get told that you aren't good enough or you get compared with someone else, you can use an internal 'whatever' and follow your own path. Your story is yours to write, and that's that.

Face Your Fears

A quick true story, not about cats, but about their distant cousins—cows and buffalo—ok, I lied about them being cousins, but the story is important. When a storm is coming, cows will stay where they are or move away from the storm, whereas buffalos will run towards it. The point is that running away from your fears makes the storm worse, as opposed to running towards your fears head-on and thus, overcoming them. The same applies to your fears of standing out, being shunned for your opinions, or being judged for dressing a certain way. Face those fears, and they will disappear (I hate to get cheesy, but the saying makes sense).

Make Your Uniqueness Positive

This category is about self-reflection, which can be a double-edged sword because it does come with an analysis of what other people say about you. I would advise using a pen and paper (maybe have two notepads in case your cat decides to plonk itself down on one). When you are ready, then write down the following:

- What do people say about me?

- How do they criticize me?

- What do I have that others don't? (my superpowers)

- What are my skills?

- What are my quirks?

Then answer all of the questions, and by the end, you will feel good about yourself as a unique individual with wonderful traits that others, especially your critics, don't possess.

You 'Ain't Gonna Please Everyone

You can't change your identity because other people question you, or because you feel that you need to please others before yourself. Nope, don't do that. It is impossible to keep everyone happy all the time, but the most important person to keep happy is your unique self. Stick to your guns, be yourself, and if people don't like it, then they have a problem, not you.

Don't Falsely Live Up to Expectations

You are you. You are unique. So, you do you. Maybe you are expected to work in the family business, but you would rather travel and explore. The latter is what you want to do, and even though your family may be disappointed, they must understand that you need to find your happiness in your own way. All you need to do is set your own expectations of yourself and live up to them...just be kind to people along the way. You would never be unkind to your cat, so why would you be unkind to people? I will leave the answer up to you, even though I am pretty certain that I know what it is.

Accept Yourself and Love Yourself

Accepting and loving yourself are ongoing processes. Besides, we all have bad habits that we can look at changing. I'm not talking about personality traits, but vices, like eating poorly or drinking too much. Flaws, on the other hand, are things that we all have, but if they don't matter to you, then other people just have to deal with it. The mechanics of self-acceptance and self-love are gradual and sustainable, so don't be too hard on yourself.

Spend Time with the Right People

If people do not appreciate your uniqueness, your quirks, and your talents, then there is no reason to hang around with them. Surround yourself with individuals that bring the best out of you, and strive to do the same for them. Like-mindedness is important because there is togetherness in spending time with like-minded people. Also, consider that people who hang out with you and tend to put you down or expose your vulnerabilities are very likely hiding their own insecurities. As the saying goes, if someone is not adding value to your life, then you don't need them.

Show Your Skills

Uniqueness is the way we act and how we do things, which is the embodiment of our personal skill set. Don't be shy to display your skills, even if they may not be well-received. Those people who don't receive your skills in an appreciative and interesting manner aren't worth worrying about. Stand up tall and show your skills to the world. If the world likes them–great. If it doesn't–no skin off your nose.

Just a quick side story–I know a guy who is an unbelievably talented opera singer, but he was always a man's man, and thought that his friends would take the mickey out of him because of his talent. He was a sports coach at an all male high school, and one day he stood up after assembly and belted out something operatic (I'm afraid I don't know many opera songs, so I couldn't tell you what it was). Anyway, it was incredible, and he got a standing ovation from the boys and staff alike. I was a pupil, and it was great to see him put his skills on show...don't be afraid to do the same.

Get Comfortable with Criticism

Some say that you shouldn't criticize what you can't understand. Just like we can't figure out why our cats ignore us, chew funny things, or sleep in tight spaces, we may not be able to figure out a particular person. Just let them be in the same way that you would like to be left to be yourself. Criticism is important and can be justified. For instance, if your behavior has hurt someone else, you need to get comfortable with that criticism, and act on it to remedy the situation or make amends. Many people go on the defensive immediately after being criticized without taking stock of the situation or giving thought to the fact that the criticism may be justified. It is okay to be criticized, and if you have to level criticism at someone else, do it as politely as possible. Often, the reason for getting the criticism was an oversight or something that the other party did without realizing that there would be harmful consequences.

Turn Comparison Into Inspiration

Comparing ourselves to each other is very common. If you make a comparison and you don't like the results, then be inspired to change those results. Success is different for everyone. For some, success is the white picket fence dream. For others, it is becoming rich. Those things are all fine, but we need to make happiness our definition of success. As normal as making comparisons is, we need to make the *right* ones.

Hold Yourself Accountable

In life, we have experiences that could have been handled differently, and let's face it, we make mistakes. We do need to hold ourselves accountable for our mistakes because they are errors that we can learn from. Accountability is fine but avoid self-judgment. Life happens, and it can be difficult and confusing, but holding ourselves accountable is a way to impose high standards and become better while maintaining our uniqueness.

If you can follow the thirteen lessons above, or at least take something away from each category, then you are on your way to loving yourself. Don't be a carbon copy of anyone else, embrace your uniqueness, just like you embrace the uniqueness (and cute strangeness) of your beloved cat or cats.

But, What Are My Talents?

I am willing to bet that you already know what your talents are, but just like you think you understand your cat, you still might have a few things to learn. There are some useful ways in which we can identify our talents, which is an exercise in promoting our unique traits with the most positive 'cattitude' possible.

Take a Life Assessment Test

What on earth is a life assessment test? You know, it's a test that assesses your life. I guess that doesn't quite answer the question, but a life assessment test is a set of statements that you read and then respond to. Most often, the test is split into four sections. Below are examples of types of questions by category:

Your Priority

On a scale of one to five. One being the lowest priority and five being the highest.

- Keeping in touch with family members

- Refrain from judging loved ones

- Give advice sincerely

Your Level of Satisfaction

On a scale of one to five. One being the lowest level of satisfaction and five being the highest.

- Amount of rest I am getting

- My body

- My personal hygiene

Your Strengths and Weaknesses

On a scale of one to five. One being the lowest and five being the highest.

- Practicing meditation

- Being a caring partner

- Leadership ability

Disc Personality

On a scale of one to 10. One being least like me and 1o being most like me.

- Aggressive and cautious

- Dynamic and driven

- Poor with routine

There are many tests available on the internet. They are all very similar and will produce correct results. So, check some of them out, take a test, and discover your talents, as well as the areas of yourself that need work.

Identify What Makes You Feel Strong

Generally, in life, the things that we are good at take less effort. As an example, someone that is good at singing just opens their mouth and belts it out. An individual that isn't such a good singer will have to think about their breathing and focus deeply on hitting each note. In this example, the former will feel strength in their talent, but because the latter does not have the same talent, they will sway to the side of weakness. Reflect on the things that make you feel strong, and pursue those talents.

Figure Out What You Spend the Most Money On

By tracking your spending, you can pinpoint where your talents lie. Perhaps you enjoy surfing, and the indicator thereof is the money you spend on surfing magazines, equipment, and surf trips. Maybe you spend most of your money on scratch toys, play mice, and the best of the best cat food...your talent is then obvious. It isn't an absolute failsafe method of identifying talent, but when combined with the other techniques in this chapter, you will know, just like your cat knows when its food is on the way.

Ask Your Friends

Your friends know you well, and if you ask them what your best and worst qualities are, they should be honest. Maybe you sing out loud a bit too often, and your monotone voice isn't always fun for everyone. On a positive quality note, you could be great at telling jokes or throwing out well-timed one-liners. Keep the best and chuck out the worst.

Ask Your Family

If your friends don't tell you that you are a bad singer, your family definitely will...your cat would, if it could talk. But here we are concerned with your interests as a child, and if your parents can point those out, then you can revisit them with enthusiasm and discover what your strengths were and could be again.

Keep a Journal

Write something down in your journal every day. Don't plan it and don't overthink it. Just put pen to paper and see what happens (I don't mean this as a metaphor, I mean it literally). After three weeks to a month, read through your journal entries and you will see patterns appearing. From this point, you can pick out your strengths and the possible realities that could become opportunities.

Look for Talent in Others

If you identify talent in other people, you can use them as inspiration. Don't be jealous because something is better than you at something. Rather see it as a challenge to develop a similar talent. There could be occasions where you realize you have more talent than another individual. For argument's sake, you read a few news articles, and you know deep down that you can do the same job, maybe even a better one, as the authors of the articles. Now that you know what your talent is, you can start making plans for your talent to work positively for you, personally.

Take Stock of Your Book, Music, and Movie Collections

These three areas of interest are very individual-based and form an expression of you as a person. Nobody has the right to criticize your tastes, and those that do so are not the kind of people you want to spend time with. Taking stock can help you supplement your identity and become a means of discovering new talents. It could also be quite fun if you come across music that you were into twenty years prior. Your cat will judge your music taste, but maybe keep it quiet when you talk to your friends if it is really embarrassing. On the other hand, if it will provide a good laugh with a small sprinkling of embarrassment, then go right ahead and share it with your cat...and your friends.

Remember Receiving Thanks

If you are being thanked on a regular basis, the trigger causing the other person or people to thank you is your talent. Maybe you are a good teacher, have admirable patience, or show commitment to your cause. If you are getting thanked (and complimented) in these regards, then you must consider them as talents. Often we brush off a thank you or go into modesty mode, but enjoying the praise is definitely acceptable too.

Be Open to Change

You could uncover your talent and then need to reshuffle some areas of your life to take advantage of that talent. Change can be scary. Just ask all those cats with butter on their feet after you move house. But change for the better is good. Don't procrastinate. Rather make the change, fearlessly, with individuality and maximize your talents.

Be Selective About Your Talents

Most of us have more than one talent, but if we have four or five, we can risk spreading ourselves thin across the spectrum of our talents. It may be a wise choice to focus on one, two, or maybe even three talents. That way, your individuality can shine, and you will be able to master the areas in which your talents lie.

Upgrade

NO! I do not mean get a new cat...unless your current one, two, or maybe even three of them could use another member on the cat team. When you have found your talent or talents, you can work on upgrading them. Perhaps you discover that you have a musical ear, and you decide to augment that talent by learning an instrument. Practice means improving your talent, and you can do so by–you guessed it–practicing. But you can also watch videos, read articles, and learn about the history of your instrument as a way of upgrading your talent. It can, and should be, an ongoing endeavor.

Reach Perfection

We can't all be as perfect as our cats are, but we can work towards perfection in our own unique, talent-rich way that can inspire ourselves and others. To be fair, what do you do after you reach perfection? Don't worry about it. You never will in the eyes of your furball buddies. Yes, they love you, but we all know that they are way closer to perfection than us mere humanoids. The point is that we need to keep making forward progress.

Find Your Passion

Eating, sleeping, nuzzling, scratching, stretching, and catching mice and birds. There is no need to continue, but if only it were that simple for us humans. So, I guess we have to stalk on...get it? Anyway, living life without a passion can leave us feeling a bit empty. My bet is that you have a passion, or more than one, but you may not realize it. What follows are some tips that will help you identify your passion or passions if they already exist. They will also help you find your passion or passions if you haven't done so yet.

Switch Perspectives

I remember talking to an older lawyer when I was a young man. He told me that he hated his job, but the money that he made allowed him to play golf on the weekends and take regular overseas holidays. In my opinion, his views, as much as I respected them, needed a massive perspective switch. Making a lot of money is something that drives so many people, but if they had to look at the situation from a different perspective, they would understand that conformity is not compulsory. Think about it, that lawyer spends more time unhappy than happy, but if he looked at the world differently and followed a path where he worked a job that he loved, the passion would negate the hollow need for a lavish lifestyle.

The above is, of course, just an example, but it is always good to look at any situation from different angles. The ultimate goal must always be to engage in what you are passionate about. This can be difficult if you don't know what your passions are, but don't panic. We are getting there.

Discover Your Number One Human Need

Cats don't really have many needs, they are cantankerous on purpose, and we know they are just playing with us inferior humans. However, as humans, there are six vital needs, as follows:

- Certainty
- Significance
- Variety
- Love
- Growth
- Contribution

I can't make the decision for you, but whatever you identify as your driving force will inform your passion. For instance, if your human need is growth, then your passion will involve steps to grow as a human–going on courses, reading self-help material, and continuously working on yourself. If your need is contribution, then your passion will likely be helping people, charity work, military service, or other activities where you give selflessly.

Look at What You Love

I know what you're thinking, but you can't stare at those lovely, snuggly, four-legged, mysterious creatures all day. I'm talking about looking at your book collection, your music or movie preferences, and the things in your life that you genuinely have a love for. An excellent way of discovering, unearthing, or confirming your passion is by asking yourself what you could talk about for 30 minutes if asked to do so. Again, I know what you're thinking, but *other* than your feline family.

Take Note of Where You Spend Your Free Time

I still know what you're thinking, and I am aware that you spend a lot of your spare time giving love to your mini-lions, but here I am talking about things like reading. If you enjoy reading, your passions may stretch to writing and teaching. If you enjoy a bit of DIY, then you could be passionate about building or construction, and if you draw pleasure from dancing, you may have a fashion for movement and choreography.

Look For Patterns

It is human nature to identify patterns, but often when it comes to patterns in our own lives, we don't even think about them. Sit down with a pen and paper, or just on a comfy chair with your right-hand feline and break down some of the patterns in your life. Don't restrict yourself to a time frame. Go as far back as you feel is necessary. The activities or endeavors that you have repeated in the past are quite possibly the passions that you need to harness and put your unique stamp on.

The Rocking Chair Test

Do cats like rocking chairs? Who knows–that is up to the kitten-cat in question. The rocking chair test is an exercise in imagination. The idea is to picture yourself as an elderly 'you,' sitting in a rocking chair on your front porch and looking back on your life. You ask yourself the following questions:

- What are my biggest regrets?

- What do I wish I had experienced?

- What passion do I wish I had followed?

- How do I want to be remembered?

If you can really get into your mind's eye and imagine yourself rocking in that old rocking chair, then you can honestly answer the questions. The answers will reveal the things that you would tell your younger self to engage in...your passions, in other words.

Consider Your Fears

On occasion, our fears can reveal our passions. We may fear quitting our job to pursue music or to backpack through Europe. It is those fears that hold us back. Fear of failure is a big inhibiting factor. But if there is something on your mind that you really want to do, and it is a true passion, then you will succeed. Let your fears guide you in the direction of your passions.

Be Unreasonable

Would your cat plonking itself on your face and restricting your airways while you are trying to sleep be considered unreasonable? Probably not—that is just cat being cat, but often passions rise from unreasonable expectations or considerations. Often, passions are not reasonable, and by exploring them with that notion in mind, you might just ignite something unique and beautiful, for which you have a burning passion.

Step Out of Your Comfort Zone

Human achievement is typified by being placed in uncomfortable situations. We are resilient—not as much as our cat-friends, but when pushed, prodded, and placed in scenarios where the odds are against us, we can flourish and thrive. So, take a cooking class, go on a trip by yourself, or build a coffee table. Whatever it may be, make yourself uncomfortable, and I am certain you will experience positive results.

Believe in Yourself

Our cats believe in us, even though it looks like they are casting judgment our way, so we owe it to them to believe in ourselves. To do this, we can use more positive language. Don't 'wish you could,' rather 'make sure you do.' You get the message, but don't worry if you are scared or have self-doubt—that is normal. However, in the name of being passionate about finding and following your passions, you must push aside the fear and the doubt and march forward like Dick Whittington with his trusted and beloved feline companion.

Chapter Conclusion

I would say that we have gotten off to a good start—some decent preening, no furballs coughed up. Rather, we have learned about comfort in being ourselves and freeing our uniqueness without judgment. We knew that we had talents and passion, but now we know how to engage them and make great strides in our personal growth crusade. And so, the time has come to relax..sort of...you'll see what I mean, my cat-napping crew.

Chapter 2

The Art of Relaxation

Lessons from the Catnap Masters

I'm not about to tell you that self-improvement includes sleeping our days away, but we do have to make a concerted effort to develop skills that quiet our minds. Our cats are so damn good at it, so why not take some lessons from the masters. In this chapter, we will look at the many benefits of rest and relaxation, in addition to deconstructing mindfulness, especially when it comes to meditation. Then, it is onto human preening, or self-care as we human preeners call it. Right, let's go fluffy...hey, I said let's go.

Rest and Relaxation

If you are hyped all the time, in go...go...go mode, and you don't take time out for yourself to rest, relax, and recharge, you will reach burnout. There are small things and some big things that you can implement to rest your body and mind as steps to improve yourself physically and mentally. Let's have a look at some great tips that are not too difficult to implement.

Take a Break

Sometimes we need a break from a stressful activity or an activity that may not be stressful but that does take intense concentration. You don't need to take a long break. Reading a chapter or two of a book, listening to an album, or the absolute best—getting silly with your cats—mouse on string style are great options. Anything to give yourself a bit of a breather by doing something that relaxes you.

Active Relaxation

Take a slow walk, preferably in nature. There is something about a walk outdoors that relaxes us. Maybe even kicking a stone about as you walk could help. It might bring back childhood memories and a smile. If you enjoy stretching, you can engage in a stretching routine or take a yoga class. A good old-fashioned stretch is always beneficial, and the relaxed feeling afterwards is definitely a recommended one.

By the way, you could get heated yoga classes. I tried one once, and I have to say that there ain't nothing relaxing about that, but each to their own.

Focus On Your Breathing

We will look at this in the next section, but just a quick summary–deep breath in as you observe your chest rising. When your lungs reach capacity, then breathe out slowly and completely. It may help to put your hand on your chest and do some counting (1,2,3,4 as you breathe in, and 1,2,3,4 as you breathe out.)

Engage Your Creativity

You don't have to be great at drawing, painting, baking, or playing an instrument. Just do it, and enjoy it while you are busy. Okay, so you probably should be good at baking, but as they say, the proof is in the pudding. If it looks a bit dodgy but tastes great, then one hundred percent for you.

I can just imagine all you readers with flour all over and your cats sitting staring at you, thinking you are as mad as a hatter. What a funny scene, indeed!

Daydream

It is probably easier to daydream if you are a child because you have less of a conceptual understanding of reality. However, as an adult, don't be reluctant to daydream about something outrageous, like being an astronaut or performing a heart transplant. You can get really creative and let your mind come up with nonsensical scenes. It is all about getting into relaxed mode, just like your precious kitty as she snoozes, oblivious to the world around her, with the odd nose wiggle, just for cuteness.

Ditch the Tech

No, not forever, just for a few hours while you do something enjoyable. When you are engaging in your 'something enjoyable,' try to keep your mind off Instagram, Facebook, and your emails. You can even make a resolution to put your devices away at a certain time in the evening, and only take them out the next morning. For many of us, this will be difficult but when it becomes a habit and we feel less edgy without them, we can use the extra time to read or to find out about things that may interest us.

Work Breaks

Time to delve a little deeper into breaks, but this time we are talking about breaks from work, specifically. We all want to be productive humans, even though our cats have no such concerns. Work breaks help us with productivity and, believe it or not, can spike our creativity. It is the prefrontal cortex (PFC) in our brains that requires a break. The PFC is responsible for focus, logical thinking, and willpower, which are all needed to reach a goal at work.

Sitting for too long isn't good for you, and even a five-minute movement break can do wonders. Our brains can become tired, and we can suffer what experts call decision fatigue, where it becomes difficult to make decisions because our brains are temporarily worn out and need a 'brain breather.' During a work break, we can restore motivation, and kick-start our productivity again. Here are some break-taking tips:

- Take a walk and clear your mind so that you can reset your creativity.

- Observe the workings of nature.

- Change the environment that you are in to mix things up and to recharge.

- Take a cap nap, or as the weirdo humans call it, a power nap.

- Make a cup of coffee—not too many per day, please.

- Play with your cat even if he is giving you 'cattitude.' He is cute whichever way you look at it.

You can give your cat the milk, but you can't make it drink...that is an obscure reference to giving you the above tips, but leaving it up to you to put them into practice. Like the simplified but complicated brain of a cat, I can't even tell if that made sense. Never mind, let's get to matters of the mind.

Mindfulness

You may have heard of cognitive behavioral therapy or CBT. Mindfulness forms part of CBT, but before we get to mindfulness meditation, we need to define CBT, which the American Psychological Association (APA) lists as follows:

Cognitive behavioral therapy (CBT) is a form of psychological treatment that has been demonstrated to be effective for a range of problems, including depression, anxiety disorders, alcohol and drug use problems, marital problems, eating disorders, and severe mental illness. Numerous research studies suggest that CBT leads to significant improvement in functioning and quality of life. In many studies, CBT has been demonstrated to be as effective as, or more effective than, other forms of psychological therapy or psychiatric medications (APA, 2023).

Mindfulness is just one component of CBT, and can be practiced almost anywhere and without the need for a psychologist or psychiatrist. It is based on being present and offers a distraction from the stress of daily living. I am going to divide mindfulness into two categories, namely acute awareness and meditation, then proceed to explain them both in detail.

Acute Awareness

Cats don't really rush unless they are scampering away from a threat, and even then, they always end up on their feet. We humans are not quite the same. We rush around and go about our business without pausing to take in and appreciate what some may consider to be mundane.

As a simple example, you have a stifling headache, and the pain is all you can focus on. However, you get into a conversation with some friends, and your mind becomes absorbed to the point where you forget about your headache. It is still there, but the chat with your friends has distracted you from focusing on the pain. We all experience stress and worry. It is normal, but some people and cats handle it better. What am I talking about? Cats don't get stressed. Right, so some people handle stress and worry better than others. If you are not a great stress handler, you are about to become one. I would like to throw out a typical scenario and then offer an alternative.

Your alarm goes off in the morning. You give your furry friend a belly rub, and she nuzzles her head against you, then decides that she wants to go on some sort of adventure. She gives a long back-arching stretch and deftly heads downstairs to find some mischief. You start worrying about some work tasks that you are behind on and stressing about what gift to get your grandmother for her 90th (not that she really cares). Before you know it, you have become so absorbed in your thoughts that you are now running late.

You spring out of bed, march to the bathroom, put the shower on, hop in, wash as quickly as possible, then hop out again. You half-dry yourself and chuck the towel on the floor—no time to hang it up. Then it's back to the bedroom, where you dress in a hurry and head downstairs, skipping a few steps on the way. Your kitty cat looks at you longingly, and you know she is ravenous. You slow down for just a few minutes to give her the food and the love that she needs–probably in reverse order. Then it is back to the rush. Two slices of bread go into the toaster. You pop them up manually before they are even properly toasted, hurriedly slap on some peanut butter and wolf them down.

You look at your watch, probably mutter an expletive, give the last bit of love for the morning to your furry companion, and head out the door.

Next is a fast walk where you look like one of those ridiculous Olympic race-walkers that are clearly running, even though nobody ever seems to point it out. Anyway, your walk becomes an actual run, and as you round the corner, you see the bus pulling away. The next expletive is not quite a mutter, and you are frazzled to the max. You pace up and down as you wait for the next bus. When it pulls up you jump in, snatch the handrail, and begin to wonder if there is time to grab a takeaway coffee, hoping that your boss is also running late.

When you arrive at your stop, you rush out of the bus, almost sprint into the diner on the corner, nearly knock over an old man coming the other way, and gasp your order to the server. It seems as if hours pass, but eventually, you have your coffee in hand, and you make the two-minute walk to your office in just one minute. You come through the door like a hurricane, and everyone looks up from their desks as you clamber to your chair, flop yourself down, exhausted, and ready (not really) to start your work day. The only positive is that your boss is later than you. It is only 8.40 am, and you are already in a bad state as the stress of deadlines, annoying clients, and loud-chewing co-workers sets in. You may be thinking that the scenario which I have painted isn't the worst, and that many people go through the same thing every day. If so, you don't realize what impact the rushed morning has on your general well-being. When everything is calm, it augurs well for a calmer day with less stress and anxiety. So, what if I told you that it doesn't have to be this way? Yes, that's what I said, and I have a feeling that you would be prepared to listen. What follows is an explanation of how immeasurably better your rushed morning would be if you started your day slightly earlier and paid acute attention to the smaller things.

You set your alarm 30 minutes earlier than usual that night. Now, the crucial part of this plan is not to snooze your alarm, or at worst, to snooze it once. You give your furry friend a belly rub, and she nuzzles her head against you, then decides that she wants to go on some sort of adventure. She gives a long back-arching stretch and deftly heads downstairs to find some mischief (this isn't part of the plan, but it happens anyway—important to include).

You get up out of bed and have a long back-arching stretch yourself as you pay attention to the way your muscles gently release the tension. You walk slowly to the bathroom, put the shower on, and step in. You notice the warmth of the water as the droplets hit your back and make their way down your body. When you wash your hair, you massage your scalp and observe the lavender smell of your shampoo. Because you are not in a rush, you elongate your shower, and when you hop out, you take time to dry yourself. You close your eyes and fixate on the soft feeling of the towel on your skin as it absorbs the water.

When you get back to your bedroom, you carefully pick out what you want to wear. You even have time to put some music on. Hell, maybe you even dance around your room a bit, letting the notes sink into your soul. You check your watch and realize that you have time on your hands. Next, it is the downstairs walk, hitting every step on the way.

The bread slots into the toaster, you push it down, and attend to cat snuggles, feline food, and more snuggles, by which time your toast has popped. You revel in the smell as you spread the peanut butter on nice and thick. Every bite is a point of focus, and you enjoy the whole experience, from the way the peanut butter feels on your pallet to the satisfaction you find as you get your morning nourishment. There is even time for more snuggles before your cat waves you goodbye, figuratively.

While you walk to the bus stop, you feel the breeze on your face, and you smile when you look at the front yards as you walk. You examine the colors of the plants, shrubs, flowers, and trees while you think about how amazing nature really is. When you arrive at the bus stop, you sing a song in your head, and you appreciate the joys of music. The bus pulls up, and you jump on nice and slow. You do a bit of people-watching—who doesn't love that? Cats, maybe? No, no, they enjoy it too—full of endearing judgment. You smile at a few people, and the smiles are returned, making you feel warm inside.

Then it's off the bus, a short walk to the diner, and a slow drink of your coffee as you walk to the office. You absorb the aroma and enjoy the strong taste of your warm brew. As you walk inside, you notice that you are one of the first to arrive, and you take the time to chat with a colleague before excusing yourself to sit down at your desk, relaxed and ready for your day.

What you have achieved is a distraction from your mind and its negativity. The human race is naturally negative, so we have to train ourselves out of negative thought patterns. Mindful observations, as above, are part of the training. There is a flaw, unfortunately, and that is the fact that your stresses and worries will come into your mind again. However, the takeaway here is that you had an hour, maybe more, of enjoying the things that many of us take for granted. You can carry this on throughout the day and keep reminding yourself to do so. In addition, you will have a happy, healthy, relaxed, and rested friend to give snuggles and belly rubs to when you get home. Oh, by the way, try to stoke the deep focus that you experienced on the way to work for the trip home at the end of the day.

Guided Meditation

For those of you who are 'non-namaste,' 'zen-absent,' and not like Buddha, please do not be put off by the word meditation. It is

43

not 'ohm...ohm...ohm' meditation, but rather an exercise in relaxation, and deep focus, with similar results to what we have just discussed.

The other name for guided meditation is body scanning, and the technique works via a recording of a calming voice that takes you through the process. You can find these mindfulness-based meditation recordings on Spotify, Apple Music, YouTube, and any other similar platforms. They range in time, but my advice would be to start with a short one–ten or fifteen minutes should be fine. The reason for that is because the focus required is hard to maintain for lengthy periods, so you need to work up to it. As you implement these skills more often, you won't need the recording. The experience will go something like this:

Find a comfortable chair or lie on your bed in a comfortable position and relax your body as much as possible. When you are ready, you can shift your focus to your toes–keep your eyes closed, but picture your toes. Next, wiggle them around, cross the big toe with its next-door partner, and wiggle some more. Notice what it feels like as your toes dance around. There might be a breeze that cools them, and if there isn't, you can create one with your imagination. Twirl your feet as you visualize them, wave them left to right, let them lead lethargically, and observe the sensations deeply.

Move slowly up to your shins. There is no need to move them around. Rather picture them in your mind, and maybe even start thinking about how incredible the human body is. You may want to pull your feet up a bit and jiggle back and forth to create ripples on your calves. Place your legs back at rest, and continue scanning upwards. Lay your arms by your sides and picture them sinking into the bed or the sides of the chair. Make motions with your fingers, give a click or two, and listen intently to the sounds that they make.

Then switch to your stomach, and try to identify the sounds it is making from the inner works. Try to imagine a warmth in your belly rising up to your chest. Take note of the breath filling your lungs–nice and cool, making you calm and relaxed. Breathe out slowly as you observe your chest rising. Stay on this part for a while, and think how lucky you are to be able to draw breath.

Let your head sway from side to side while feeling your neck muscles stretch ever so gently. Lick your lips and enjoy the sensation as they pick up warmth and then cool down. Picture your ears and how intricate their makeup is, then focus on your hair or head. Create a warm relaxing glow in your mind, and let it fade slowly as you open your eyes, refreshed, relaxed, and calm.

Let's assume for just a moment that your tabby, ginger, or Persian doesn't decide that he or she needs to sit on your head during the guided meditation. The idea is to distract yourself to the point where you have no thoughts whatsoever floating around in your head. Very difficult! I know, but as I say, you will work up to it. What I like to do if my thoughts stray is to have three separate visions that I can call on in my mind's eye to bring me back to focus on the body scan. Personally, when my mind starts to wander, I will picture a red triangle, a breaking wave, or a bright, starry night. Those visions trigger my mind back to relative blankness, and I can get back to my task at hand.

As with the acute awareness exercise, the flaw is that your worries and anxieties still exist, but the distraction for however many minutes brings a sense of calm upon you. Being calm and relaxed is obviously beneficial in an overall manner. You can practice mindfulness meditation almost anywhere. Just avoid closing your eyes if you are engaging in activities that require looking and seeing–driving is a good example.

Chapter Conclusion

Right, listen up, all you catnappers. Don't be cat slackers, but do make time for rest and relaxation through the methods discussed in this chapter. Breaks are necessary at work or otherwise. They help us recharge our brains and get the focus re-aligned. On the subject of focus, you now have the tools through mindfulness to engage in acute awareness. In addition, mindful meditation is now your friend, and the cat choir and I encourage you to give it a good go. I know you're wondering what is coming next–don't be so curious, but be a bit curious and join me as we become adventurous.

Chapter 3

Curiosity Killed the Cat, But Satisfaction Brought It Back

Finding Adventure in Everyday Life

C ats are most definitely a curious bunch. They are curious to us humans but also curious, themselves. They like to explore, investigate, and then nap. Well, eat and then nap. There is a certain amount of curiosity that touches us, but often we shy away from pursuing things that puzzle us. Sometimes we don't even realize how much stuff we can be curious about. In this chapter, I will show you how to embrace your curiosity. Doing so is a great opportunity to increase your general knowledge and become a more interesting person, leading to better interpersonal relationships and more social interactions. You can't only talk to your cat. She will definitely get bored and go on an expedition. Not because you're boring, just because she is a cat and cats do cat things. Before we get cracking, remember that asking why is always a good thing, as is asking how.

Trying New Things

If you have ever caught yourself saying, 'I wonder what (insert activity) is like,' then you have considered trying something new or different. We have talked about finding our passions and stepping out of our comfort zones, but maybe we need an extra push to do so. You are about to get excited about some of the reasons to try some of the new things that you may be curious about. Maybe you will even discover some motivation to *find* things to be curious about.

Finding Fulfillment

Learning the guitar is a really good example. So many people say that they wish that they could play the guitar. However, when they are asked why they don't try, the answer is often that they are not musical. Firstly, tone deafness is a myth, and secondly, playing a musical instrument is about teaching your fingers, in the case of guitar and piano, where to go and when. It's just muscle memory, as is the case with learning to drive a car, hit a golf ball, or get up on a surfboard.

Imagine if you just gave it a go. Throw caution to the wind and let your curiosity run free. Perhaps you will discover that playing the guitar is not for you, but without acting on your curiosity, you may never have known. Who knows, you may get to be one of the pussy cats in Josie and the Pussycats.

A Greater Sense of Appreciation

It can be really refreshing to learn about other cultures through different foods, customs, or languages. Maybe after reading this, you will be motivated to find out about people that are different from you. Even if it isn't a cultural thing, when you meet someone and you show genuine curiosity in them, the scene is set for a good conversation where you both learn something. Sometimes the strangeness of others makes you appreciate yourself. To be clear, strange to me might be normal to you, so it is all relative. In any event, we should all try to take note of the things we are appreciative of.

Building Confidence

Cats are generally confident, or maybe they just don't care. Both are good traits—we shouldn't

worry about what others think of us. But, if we look
into every curiosity that we have, our confidence
can grow because we broaden our minds. Learning
something new or gaining knowledge on a subject
that you are interested in really are virtues in life.
There is also no foul in self-praise. When you do
something well or you reach a small goal, then
take some time to acknowledge what you have
achieved, and see your confidence grow.

You Could Discover Your Purpose

Have you ever heard the expression that someone
has missed their calling? Whether yes or no, I
will explain. Perhaps you are an accountant, and
you really don't like it, but one day you decide
to build a coffee table out of a pallet just to
find out if it is possible. You do an excellent
job, and everyone that comes to your house
comments on what a lovely coffee table you have.
Missing your calling, in this case, would have been
becoming an accountant rather than a carpenter
or tradesperson. So, what do you do? It's obvious.
You do what your cat would tell you to do–change
professions–you have discovered your purpose,
and it can change your life. Had you not been
curious, you may have remained in a job that did
not bring you joy for the rest of your working life.

Your purpose is driven by passion and vice-versa. If you were not curious before, I would venture to say that you are now.

By the way, it is possible to build a coffee table out of a pallet. Mine was so wonky that it collapsed when my cat tip-toed daintily across it. Conclusion–carpentry is not my calling.

Likes and Dislikes

If you don't try, you will never know. I am aware that you know that, but if you are not curious about things, you will struggle to tell your likes from your dislikes. Maybe you have your mind made up that you only like non-fiction, but someone convinces you to try out a John Grisham novel. You absolutely love the book, and a whole new world of fiction opens up its doors for you. I would say that bungee jumping and skydiving are probably things that you can decide against without trying to make sure. Your call–you do you.

Make a Memory

Okay, make more than one memory, but try to make satisfying ones. Like the rocking chair example, think about what your regrets would be if you don't get curious and don't go on adventures. If you are really daring, you can write down five new things to try, throw them in a hat, and pick one. Please do not apply this to your cats...you shouldn't have favorites. With great memories comes wonderful reminiscing with people who made the memories with you. This can become addictive, just like bird-chasing is addictive to the 'you know whos.' Exploring your curiosity really does make you a more well-rounded human being, not that Screech the cat will notice.

Meeting New People

Maybe you are curious about weightlifting, bodybuilding, or curling–pretty much out-of-the-box activities. Chances are that if you tried one of them out, you would meet people that don't move in the same circles that you do. My bet is that you will get acquainted with some interesting people that you can learn a lot from, and hopefully, you can also teach them a few interesting things–a type of mutual curiosity. Maybe bodybuilding is your calling, as we discussed previously. Find out if you can bring your cat convoy to the Olympics as a starting point.

Coming Out of Your Shell

Diving into your curiosity puts you in situations that you may ordinarily not have embraced. Let's say you decide to join an amateur drama society. That could be super scary, but when you get into it, you will become more confident and may be on your way to joining the Screen Actors Guild. Your first role could be in the motion picture version of Cats, hehe, haha. You will find fulfillment as you come out of your shell and explore the many treats that life can bring when curiosity is engaged.

You Will Have a Better Concept of Fear

Most things are scary the first time we try them, but without going through with things, we will never find the fulfillment that they may bring. Our minds are really good at maximizing our fears, especially the fear of the unknown. It feels really good to overcome a fear, and when you try a new activity and overcome the fear that you have, or should I say the concept of the fear that you have, then fear becomes more relatable. You can then manage your fears in future endeavors, which shows a good sense of control as a human. This would be nothing like the sense of control (lack of) over your cat.

The Appreciation of Time

Cats aren't concerned about time, and frankly, a lot of humans aren't either, but we should be. Our lives go by so fast, and an appreciation of time when you do something new is a wonderful thing. Back to the guitar-learning example–it is something that you improve at very slowly, but you will appreciate your improvements so much more. In addition, you will appreciate the fact that you became curious and dedicated time as a result of your curiosity.

It's Healthy for Your Brain

A very sad fact of life is that many people retire and they stop living because their brains just become inactive. Whether young or old, we have to keep our brains active, and while curiosity is the first step, acting on curiosity is the part that invokes activity. Being able to think about things daily is a path to living a more fulfilling life.

You Experience More of Life and Become More Interesting as a Person

Getting out of a routine and exploring things, as well as putting yourself into new experiences, means that you, well, experience life a bit more than the next cat. It also gives you more to talk about, which generally means that you are perceived as interesting. Okay, not only perceived as interesting, you *are* interesting...as interesting as your cat? Never!

Humility

New experiences give you different perspectives and give you a sense of how unimportant we are in this world. Without a doubt, our feline buddies are way more important than us. We begin to understand that we are all on this planet doing our best and that we all have hardships. Being humble is an excellent trait, and it is something that is difficult to fake. Feeding our curiosity and discovering more about ourselves, others, and the world in general brings that true, genuine humility.

Quickfire Curiosity

All of the above reasons for curiosity are equally as good as the next, but maybe you need to ease into it. A cat ain't going to do a marathon, and the above reasons could be seen as a marathon. You might want to do a marathon, but let's look at the following ways to improve your curiosity as a sprint. Can you imagine Garfield the Cat doing a sprint? Just the thought of it would make him need to take a nap.

Pump up the Passion

I'm sure you know the one about doing a job you love and it not feeling like work. Let's deal with that first. If you aren't enjoying your job, you should check what's out there. A bit of window shopping won't hurt, so feed your curiosity, and maybe you will find something that you are passionate about and turn it into a career. To build on the 'doing a job you love' gambit, if you practice your passions, life will be fulfilling. That's all.

Ask Questions

If you meet someone new or you are stuck in a queue, it won't hurt to strike up a conversation and ask a lot of questions. Many people like talking about themselves. After all, it is the subject each one of us knows the most about. Curiosity creates questions, and in turn, the questions create connections that could be long lasting and enriching to your life.

Be the Teacher and the Pupil

If you are passionate about something, then get your friends involved. Maybe you decide to take up ultimate frisbee, and you go for a few lessons. In that scenario, you are the pupil, and when you offer to teach your friends, you are the teacher. Fifi, the cat, does not count as a pupil, by the way.

Mastery

You may have heard of the 10,000-hour theory, which hypothesizes that you need to put in 10,000 hours of work to master something. That would indicate that you have to start pretty young and stick to whatever it is you want to master. If you had to dedicate three hours per day to an activity, it would take about seven years to reach mastery. Our cats have three hours per day, but they are masters at all things catty already. We are unlikely to be able to find three hours daily, but we can master the basics of something like cooking, CrossFit, or cannonballing. If I'm honest, I used 'canon balling' for the triple C effect. You can replace it with piano, drums, hockey, cycling, pick-up sticks, magic, or anything else that your heart desires. Once you know the basics, you can really start having fun. My advice is to try out a few things, learn the basics, and see what happens.

Takin' a Walk

Going for a walk can help your curiosity via observation, and it is also healthy, plus it clears your mind, leaving room to get curious. On your walk, you can activate your senses—smell the flowers, feel the breeze, hear the children playing, taste the bark (maybe), and see everything in your vicinity.

Understand Your Enemy

That sounds a bit war-like, but what I mean is that if there are social opinions that you disagree with, then delve a bit deeper into what social commentators are saying. It may be something to do with heavy issues like Roe vs. Wade or transgender teenagers for instance, but if you get curious about the argument made by the other side, you will be a richer person for it.

Explore

Be a tourist in your own town...or city. You may be surprised about how much history your town or city has. Take an afternoon, go to the tourist bureau, grab a map and a to-do guide, and explore. It would be amazing to have some interesting facts that you can share at dinner parties. You can even practice by telling your cat and chuckling at his confused and slightly condescending facial expressions.

Reflect

Not like a cat pawing at its own reflection in the mirror, but rather an examination of self.

Reflection can give us a better understanding of our disposition and help us identify why we do certain things. Let us label this one 'self-curiosity.' So many of us don't even fully understand ourselves, and self-curiosity is a potential remedy for this. Reminder—be honest with yourself even if you have to admit faults.

Curiosity and Science

A scientist will find anything to study, and curiosity is on the list marked 'anything to study.' The curiosity research project was carried out by two doctoral students at the University of Buffalo. One of the findings was as follows:

Highly curious individuals tend to experience more positive interpersonal outcomes than the less curious in different social contexts as a function of the way they process rewarding or 'appetitive' stimuli during the relationship process (Kashdan & Rose, 2002).

That sentence is scientifically confusing, so let me simplify it. In social situations, let's say a group conversation, people that are very curious leave the conversation feeling more fulfilled than those who are less curious.

The study also found that curiosity is a factor that influences learning environments. It does make sense in a way, as it indicates that the person in the classroom asking the most questions is likely to take away more from the lesson than the others. One could forgive a bit of cynicism on this one. However, we are more concerned with personal development, so a quick thank you to the people in the white lab coats before we move on.

New Interests or Hobbies

In addition to the examples of things to get curious about, I would like to give you some ideas of the best interests, or hobbies if you like, for building confidence and growing self-improvement. In addition to self-improvement, you will be spending your time constructively, instead of passing time at home with activities such as channel hopping, gaming, or scrolling through the negative feeds that social media provides.

Puzzles

Remember those rainy days when you were a kid and your parents whipped out a 1,000 piece puzzle? It seemed boring at first, but as you got more into it you found the inspiration to take up the challenge and aim to get to the end, hoping that the final piece was actually the final piece. Well, that can happen again, start with a small puzzle and see if you enjoy it. There is something simple and special about the concentration required to complete what appears to be a pretty easy task, but one that can also be complex and challenging.

Artwork

Get curious about painting, or knitting, or...and this is a cool one, miniature ship building. You can find miniature ship building kits at educational toy shops. They consist of a whole bunch of small wooden components that come together to make a mini ship. There is glue, instructions, and a picture of the final product to keep you inspired. Make sure you put some sort of barrier in place so your beloved furry tornado cat does not knock your creation over!

Learn a Language

You never know, you might be really good at it, plus it gives you something to talk about–in your native language at first, but hopefully in your second language at some point. There are plenty of language learning apps and online courses that can help you through the learning process. It does require time and concentration, but feeding your curiosity and having a cathartic experience are big wins for personal growth.

Take a Solo Trip

Have a weekend to yourself, make a rough plan, and go on an exploratory journey. This will offer some good 'me time.' First, make sure you assign someone to take care of your cat, or even better, bring him along for that unconditional (sort of) companionship. It would be an achievement if you put away your laptop, phone, tablet, and any other devices for a weekend of clarity and mind-cleansing.

Write a Memoir

Writing about yourself and your experiences can be very liberating, even if you chuck your scribblings away afterwards. If you decide to keep them, maybe you will be a best seller one day–a great subject for day dreams. Perhaps write a few poems, something satirical maybe, involving cats, but with an important message. I can't quite think of where you could find inspiration. Oh wait, the cat kingdom, of course.

Cook...Without a Recipe

Clear the kitchen, give the cat a toy, hide the recipe books, explore the cupboards, and whip something up with what you have. You could even get a friend involved, for observational and company-keeping purposes, or to give you some tips. I am aware that your cat-friend will be there, but here, I am talking about inviting a human-friend.

Volunteer

It may be as simple as an hour or two on a Saturday morning to do a beach cleanup in a group that does various volunteering based activities. You will be doing some good, which will make you feel good about yourself. You will meet new people and perhaps find ways to help out in other areas, such as teaching English to refugees, or taking disabled children on trips to the beach or the park. Giving selflessly is an excellent way to do good and feed the soul at the same time.

Chapter Conclusion

No cats were killed. In fact, no cats were harmed in any way while exploring curiosity in this chapter. It is safe to say that becoming curious informs the idea of stepping out of our comfort zones, but the same is true of the reverse. Curiosity gives us depth, makes us more interesting, augurs well for fulfillment, and enriches our lives. There are so many advantages to feeding our curiosity, and if we actively do so, then we can improve our confidence and find our purpose in life. We open ourselves to new experiences, including meeting new people. On top of that, curiosity is healthy for our brains, and improved well-being is a positive collateral. You need to ask questions, have discussions, discover your passions, and spend some time on reflection. If you ever doubt the positivity that curiosity breeds, just think of those good old scientists that used big words to confirm it...thanks again, scientists, but a word of warning—never touch my cat! Following on from that stern warning, let's move on to talk about talking.

Chapter 4

Mastering the Art of Communication

How to Speak Your Mind Like a Cat

L et's be honest with ourselves, our cats rule the roost, they run the household, and they do whatever they please. It actually might be a good thing that cats can't talk because if they could, the result would probably be ridiculing their humans. To our cats, we are just silly, but they still love us unconditionally, or at least we think they do...time to get the scientists onto that one. Anyway, I seem to be rambling, but what I am getting at is that if cats did talk, they would not mince their words. They would eat the mince, thank us for it in a sarcastic way, and then speak their minds. I did say mince, but mice would probably work too. There are no human social codes that apply to the cat world, and it would be great if the two-legged individuals that make up human society could just speak their minds with no fear of recourse. We are slightly restricted by politeness and compliance, but we can learn the subtleties of speaking our minds when the time is right. Good communication is important in establishing and maintaining relationships, as well as taking care of the second most important being after the cats—ourselves. In this chapter, we will deconstruct effective communication in different settings, and we will come out better people for it on the other side.

Small Talk

Argh! Don't we all hate small talk?! I guess it depends on the situation, and small talk is just part of life. We could call it the boring...ish precursor to a good conversation. Well, a *possible* good conversation. You get some people that are natural conversationalists and others that experience social anxiety, or otherwise are just rude or indifferent. Confidence is key, and it is something that can be learned. You may think that small talk is not necessary to address because it is just frivolous chat to stave off awkwardness. You would be correct in a way. However, if you become good at small talk, your confidence will become apparent. I said confidence, not arrogance, keep that in mind. Starting with small talk is starting at the beginning, and there are some useful lessons to be learned.

We will start with the innocuous kind of small talk that you exchange with a server, a cashier, a petrol attendant, or someone in the service industry, when the interaction will be a short one. Generally, it is only pleasantries that are exchanged, for example, you are ordering a takeaway coffee:

You: 'Hello, how are you today?'

Server: 'I'm fine thanks, what can I get for you?'

You: 'Cappuccino please.'

Server: 'Coming right up.'--hands cup to you–'here we go, have a nice day.'

You: 'Thanks very much, enjoy your day.'

These sorts of small talk conversations happen on a daily basis, and there is a script of sorts. When we ask someone how they are doing in these scenarios, we don't expect a detailed story, in the same way that we would if the question was directed at a friend.

I did say it is about confidence. Thus, asking and answering the 'very small talk' questions should be done with conviction. Also, be polite, even though the chat is kind of mandatory, politeness gets noticed.

If the small talk required is a bit deeper than the above interaction, the usual frivolous, but slightly less frivolous than the above, will apply. At a birthday, you could ask how a person knows the birthday boy, talking about the weather is always an option, or saying something to do with current affairs. I don't need to spell it out for you. The important thing is to establish a connection, even if it is a shallow one at first, and from there you are C for cat, I mean A for away.

Body Language

We can all read the body language that our cats use, but how much emphasis do we put on interpreting the body language of other people during conversations? Probably more than you think—a lot of body language interpretation is subconscious. Wow, I feel like I keep using the term body language, but I don't know how else to put it! There are some absolutely fascinating facts about body language, so let's have a quick butcher's hook (look) at the 'factoids,' and proceed from there.

Research has told us that our thoughts are evidenced by our body before popping into our minds (Lenhardt, 2016). The delay is only nanoseconds, but it is incredible nonetheless.

Another interesting body language fact is that women have a wider peripheral vision than men do. This facilitates a subtle, pretty much non-noticeable scan of a man's body. This is why women don't really ogle, as opposed to men, but the only reason is that male peripheral vision is limited, meaning that men will look at a woman up and down, most often, with a very obvious giveaway (Lenhardt, 2016).

I could write a whole book containing these interesting tidbits, but we are not here only for such purposes, so I'll give you one more before continuing.

If two people start a conversation toe to toe, and one of the participants moves his or her feet slightly away, or in an outward direction, such is a sign of disagreement (Lenhardt, 2016).

Heck, I actually forgot to give you a definition of body language, just like your cat 'forgot' to give you snuggles. Here we go:

The gestures, movements, and mannerisms by which a person or animal communicates with others.

Yup, animal is included in that definition. I guess we are animals, mammals at least, but it is interesting to note that animal interactions are part of the definition. However, if we look at it another way, it is pretty kit-cat-cool that we share so much communication convention with our four-legged furry rascals. I'm talking about our cats, but you can interpret the furry part widely.

Sadly, there are people who study body language, with nefarious intentions. There are theories that mimicking the movements of others can sub-consciously coax them into forming a connection with you. Once that connection is created, it becomes easier to manipulate the other person to get a business deal, a sexual experience, or a subtly coerced revelation of something ultra-personal. We are not here for that nonsense, but I do have some tips for you to optimize your body language in the name of politeness, friendliness, integrity, and honesty.

Look the Person in the Eyes

Let's first get one thing out of the way. In some cultures it is rude to look someone in the eyes. So, if you plan to travel to a different country or area, be sure to find out about that! In the States, as is the case with many parts of the world, it is considered rude if you don't look a person in the eye. I'm not talking about a staring contest, even though we know that the winner would be of the feline persuasion. I'm talking about looking the person in the eye, and breaking gaze every now and then. Doing so, gives off the signs of confidence and respect. It is quite noticeable if someone avoids eye contact, and I would encourage everyone to pay attention to the courtesy of eye contact. A quick confession–I wanted to say that there is a feline between eye contact and staring, then say that I meant fine line, but I thought it was too cheesy...maybe you should decide, but as long as you get the eye contact message, I will be happy.

Give a Firm Handshake

A firm handshake is a sign of confidence and self-assuredness. Don't squeeze so tightly that you break a bone in the other person's hand. Just nice and firm while looking the person in the eye, hold for a second, and then release. Avoid standing with your hands at your sides. Rather thrust out your hand first as the initiator, and you will establish some body language to create rapport before the conversation starts.

Good Posture

This is something that you should work on as it is, from a body health point of view. But leaving that aside, it is your aim to stand up straight, with your shoulders back. Other people will pick up the positive body language that good posture promotes, and you will feel more confident as the body language bounces back and forth. Sitting hunched over or standing with your shoulders drooping down do not portray an image that garners interest from others.

Stand a Reasonable Distance Apart

Although we love affection from our cats, there are those times, mostly after a meal (the cat's meal, not yours), when their breath doesn't smell the best. Think of this when you are meeting someone and then having a discussion. It's not only that, though. Standing too close can make the situation slightly awkward. On the other side of the coin, don't stand so far apart that you have to shout small talk at each other.

Smile

Don't throw out fake smiles, but allow yourself to smile in a genuine way. This creates warmth and gives the other person an inclusionary feeling. Generally, if this is the case, the feeling flows both ways, leading to a comfortable chat, where curiosity can be engaged, and personal growth triggered. A bit of a fun one before we carry on–here are nine smile facts that you may find interesting:

- When we smile, endorphins are released (that is why it is so pleasurable watching our cats, shaking our heads in an endearing way, and flashing a smile across our faces).

- Smiles are contagious–okay, you probably knew that one.

- As babies, smiling is the first expression we learn.

- Smiling can pick up your mood,

- Monkeys, apes, and chimpanzees are also smilers, just like humans (cats are way too cool to throw a smile our way).

- Smiling makes you more approachable.

- Children smile more than adults—we should take more cues from the kiddos.

- There are 19 different types of smiles (yes, you can Google that).

- Smiling can boost your immune system.

It is very difficult to avoid smiling back when someone smiles at you—try it.

Body Language to Avoid

Everyone has their own way of standing or sitting, but we want to avoid being closed off during conversations. Before we get to the 'don'ts' of body language, one being staying off your phone during conversations, here is the conclusion of a pertinent study:

Eighty-nine percent of cellphone owners said they had used their phones during the last social gathering they attended. But they weren't happy about it; 82 percent of adults felt that the way they used their phones in social settings hurt the conversation.

Right, so we have covered the cellphone thing. Here are the rest of the don'ts:

- Too much eye contact—it creates

awkwardness–a balance needs to be struck.

- Crossing your arms or legs–this makes you appear closed off.

- Looking at your watch.

- Nodding excessively–this makes it look as if you are trying to hurry the other person along.

- Fidgeting.

- Frowning.

I don't want you to over-analyze all that is body language, just like I don't want you to over-analyze your cat's weird behavior. Don't worry; Kitty McCatsnap thinks you're weird too. The above are just some things to look out for that may be inhibiting your ability to have more meaningful conversations.

The Talking Bit

Remember when I said that the moment you stop engaging your brain is the moment when you start to age? No? Fair enough, I didn't put it quite like that, but at the end of the day, it is our social interactions and conversations that stimulate our brains. You definitely remember the dopamine part though. No? Just joking, we haven't got there yet, but you probably know a bit about dopamine already. It is the hormone that our brain produces when we experience something pleasurable. Chocolate, sex, and exercise are the most commonly quoted dopamine-triggering events. However, good conversations are also dopamine producers, and dopamine certainly contributes to living our best lives.

The Importance of Conversations

Conversations are key to growth, development, and overall happiness. Meaningful conversations have an incredibly significant impact on maintaining healthy relationships; relationships that encourage rather than discourage, and relationships that are permanent rather than temporary (Carbril, n.d.).

Emily Carbril's statement speaks for itself. She is a writer for the Long Walks blog, and the above is an extract from her article, *Why Meaningful Conversations Are Important For Our Relationships.* With emphasis on relationships, we need to remember that human connection allows for the personal growth that Carbril talks of. Think back to the best date you've ever been on or the first time you fell in love – conversation was abounding, and it made you feel great – well, my catty companions, that is what we are aiming at. It seems appropriate at this point to look at ways in which we can have deeper, more meaningful, and fulfilling discussions that help facilitate living our best lives.

Listening Versus Hearing

In one ear and out the other is what we sometimes think when we talk to our feline buddies, and they most likely think the same when they stare at us. There is a difference between listening and hearing. The latter is taking in the sound of someone's voice, but concentrating on something else or not at all, whereas listening comprises hearing and processing what you hear. A great way to do so, which also leads to better conversations, is active listening.

Active listening is characterized by asking clarifying questions or giving prompts for continued discussions. By doing so, you show the other person or people that you are invested in the conversion. The following active listening phrases serve as accurate examples:

- That is interesting, but I just want to check

that I understood it correctly. Were you saying that your cats can do cartwheels? (silly topic, but a bit of fun)

- If I understand you correctly, your opinion is X, Y, and Z.

- I'm sorry to interrupt, but I just want to be sure that...

- I'm not sure what I would have done in that situation; what do you think?

Repeating parts of what you have heard back to the person talking, so you can clarify what they said is also part of active listening. People appreciate others doing this, as again, it shows investment in the conversation.

Listening with Empathy

Empathy is defined as follows:

The action of understanding, being aware of, being sensitive to, and vicariously experiencing the feelings, thoughts, and experience of another of either the past or present without having the feelings, thoughts, and experience fully communicated objectively.

The way to show empathy is linked to a few things, curiosity being one of them, and we all know the benefits of being curious. If someone is opening up about something personal, asking questions can result in greater empathy as you begin to relate on a deeper level. You will invariably be able to identify similarities in experiences, and conveying them to the other participant(s) in the discussion will show your sincerity. Below are five empathy-inducing statements and questions for you to use:

- Thank you for sharing that information. It must have been difficult for you.

- I can relate to what you are going through.

- It may be easier to give up, but please keep going, and I will be here for you.

- You are doing the best you can. Always remember that.

- How did you feel when that happened?

Patience

I can guarantee that we have all experienced situations where we have something to contribute to a conversation, and we anticipate a pause so that we can jump in and cast our wisdom forth.

Doing so means that you are not listening intently enough, as your focus is on yourself. Exercising some patience by making sure that you are fully present will stand you in good stead to be part of a productive and fulfilling discussion.

Trustworthiness

Our cats can trust us, and we would never let them down. In this regard, we should take a good lesson out of our own books and apply it to human interaction. Trust is something that we need to prove, but if someone conveys information to us in confidence, we must make sure we are trustworthy enough to keep it confidential. Being transparent, offering help, and not talking about how amazing you are should send a message of transparency. Please feel free to talk about how amazing your cat is—that line of discussion is perfectly acceptable.

Self-Control

Don't hijack the conversation, and don't jump to conclusions before blurting something out that is incorrect or insensitive. Keep in mind that if you dominate the discussion, keep interrupting, and don't let others get a word in, then those others are unlikely to have further conversations with you. Be kind, patient, and helpful. Nuff said.

Saying No

Our cats will do exactly what they want to do without letting anyone–human or animal–stand in their way. It is more challenging to do this on two legs, and many of us are people pleasers. We cut off our noses to spite our faces, and place the happiness and well-being of others before our own. Life being life, there are many things that we have to do, but if we have a choice, we are allowed to be a little bit selfish when making decisions.

This might sound strange at first but bear with me. What did he say? Does he have a bear with him? It would be better if it was a cat. I guess I should stop talking to myself and about myself at the same time and get on with it...I'll start again–this might sound a bit strange, but have an open mind. There is a technique that allows us to say 'no' with conviction and confidence. It is called the 'yes, no, yes' technique and it is not as strange as one may think.

The first yes is saying 'yes' to yourself, as in choosing what *you* want to do. This is an internal affirmation of the 'y' word–not out loud. As an example, you are at work, busy as can be, and your manager gives you a task. You know that you are already thinly spread and that there is an incredibly slim chance that you will get the task done to the best of your abilities. Now, stay with me. Your internal yes is like a yes to the no. What I mean is that you say 'yes' to not being able to complete the task. Next up is your confident, out loud 'no.' But you follow it up with an out loud yes. To simplify it, here is how the conversation would go from your side:

No, I am not able to take on the task now because I am inundated. If I agree to execute the task, I will not be equipped to give it my full attention, meaning that my other work will suffer. If you give me two days to finish up what I am currently busy with, then I am quite prepared and willing to take the task on.

The last offering is the second yes, in the 'yes-no-yes' method. The end result is that you have looked after your own interstates first but have come up with a viable solution. You are not shirking responsibility, and if it is a genuine case of inundation, the offer to do what you have been asked to do in a few days will be taken as a willingness to get around an obstacle.

Exiting a Conversation

There are many reasons for needing to leave a conversation. You may have an appointment to get to, or perhaps something in the chat has made you feel uncomfortable, but you still want to be polite. It is definitely better to leave a conversation gracefully than clumsily. Let's face it, very few people are as interesting as our sleepy-eyed cats, and some conversations may become boring. Whatever your reason for wanting to exit a conversation, the below tips should come in handy:

- Have some exit lines ready, such as 'it was great to meet you, and I don't be rude, but I must excuse myself.'

  – There isn't even a need to give a reason–nobody can argue with the above politeness.

- Don't fidget or look flustered. Stay calm, and excuse yourself when you get a gap to do so.

- If you are at a function, there are opportunities to say things like, 'it has been great chatting, but I need to catch up with Caroline the cat, perhaps we can reconvene a bit later' (maybe leave out the part about Caroline being a cat unless she is a function-attending feline).

- You can bring the conversation to a close by summing it up or directing the chat in a direction that will close the discussion loop and allow you to exit.

- You could say, 'It has been great chatting. I need to head home to feed my cats, but I will find you on Facebook.'

– Follow through on your spoken intention. If you don't do so, you will look a little silly if you run into that person again.

– This example assumes that you are talking to someone who you recently met.

At the end of the day, you must aim for tactfulness, politeness, and gracefulness–like Caroline, of course.

Chapter Conclusion

Now that you are a conversation expert, we can stalk on forward, jump in, and land on our feet. But first, a few reminders. Small talk is inevitable, and you now have the tools to get really good at it. Body language plays a massive part in conversation, and looking someone in the eyes while issuing a firm handshake is great body language that starts a conversation. Smiling helps a lot and must be maintained through the talking bit of the discussion. Listen actively, be patient, lay yourself bare in an honest manner, and say no when you need to. Ah yes, and finally, leave a conversation gracefully, just like we will exit this chapter and prance up onto the catwalk. Alright, kitty-cat lovers, follow me on the path to further personal growth.

Chapter 5

Confidence is Key

Lessons from the Catwalk

I guess that is why the runway type of structure that models walk up and down is called a catwalk. Why? Because cats have supreme confidence, and to prance around in high heels in front of a bunch of people that you don't know, takes confidence. Don't panic, I am not going to throw you onto any form of stage, but I am going to give you some useful lessons in developing, well not developing but rather uncovering your confidence. In this chapter, you will learn how to build more confidence, overcome self-doubt, and create an ongoing culture of positive thinking. We will then roll them all into one cotton ball and let our cats playfully paw at the cotton.

Ways to Build Confidence

To some, confidence is natural, to others, it is a work in progress, and a lot of people are really good at faking it. Then you get arrogance, and in the case of people that are highly successful, confidence can cross the bridge to arrogance. We notice this quite a bit in sports. To be the best at something, you have to have huge levels of self-confidence, and a certain amount of arrogance. The latter is not the worst thing as long as it can be backed up, and let's face facts, the kitten-catten world is full of arrogant little furry faced balls of cuteness. Confidence can definitely be learned and it can also be coaxed out. We are going to look at some different methods to get your confidence up, or increase its efficacy if it is already there.

Get Things Done

It feels pretty good to put a big tick next to the items on your to-do list after you have done them. Even if it is a normal everyday activity like getting groceries, making a phone call, or sending an email, there is a sense of achievement, which is enhanced if you have a checklist that is written down using the old-fashioned pen and paper method. I would encourage readers to go out and get a notebook, preferably one with cute cats on it. When you get home, pet your cat, draw a picture of a cat on the first page of the notebook, then write down the things that need to get done. One of the 'to-do' items could be to start exercising–an excellent example. Starting an exercise regime can boost self-confidence in a big way, especially if you hit health and weight goals. Let's say you decide to run five miles three times a week. Writing it down makes it more real, and gives you a sense of accountability to yourself. Be specific–if your three exercise days are Monday, Wednesday, and Friday, you want to write down '5-mile run' on each day, and then tick or cross it off when you complete each run. On some days you really won't feel like pounding the pavement after work. You would rather have kitty cuddles, and there is no problem with that part, but you should try to incorporate a bit of both. On the running front, do something at least, even if it is a mile and a half. You have still achieved something, and adjusting the run length in your book before ticking it off still stokes a sense of achievement from which confidence emerges. Improving yourself in any way is a confidence booster, and anyone can do it with a few pen strokes and some self-discipline.

Just to be clear, it doesn't have to be running, the premise applies to any goal. The better you get at hitting small goals, the more chance there is that you will hit bigger ones, which notches up confidence to another level.

Monitor Your Progress

This is a bit of a continuation of ticking off things from a list, but it applies in a wider sense. It doesn't matter what you are trying to achieve, quantifying your progress in increments applicable to the situation gives you a sense of satisfaction as you move forward. If you are looking for a new job, you can take stock of how many resumes you have managed to send out. You can quantify how many jobs your skills match, or how many interviews you have been to. It is also helpful to make notes on how you can learn from mistakes, or from lessons that you have been taught in pursuit of your goal. Back to the exercise routine–recording the time it takes you to run 5 miles, and then trying to beat that time, will fill you with pride when it happens. When you look back on any journey and how far you have come, your confidence is bound to spike.

Do the Right Thing

Being human means being exposed to temptation, but unlike our cats, who are too cute to be **catstegated**, I mean castigated, there are ramifications for acting in a way that goes against our standards and values. There is no excuse for doing something just because we can get away with it, and unless we are complete psychopaths, we have consciences that should keep us in check. When we have done something wrong and our consciences kick in, we feel bad or guilty or develop a sense of regret. These emotions can spiral, and in extreme cases, we cultivate self-hate, which does no favors for confidence. We know it is wrong to steal, cheat on one's spouse, or pass blame for an act that we committed onto another person. The staggering thing is that we still engage in these activities, and we don't learn. Act as if a TV crew is following you and filming your daily activities for a documentary. This will help you do the right thing, and to uphold your morals, thus avoiding a dent in your confidence. Finding someone's wallet with money in it and managing to track them down, followed by returning the wallet without taking the money is an example of doing the right thing. You feel good, they feel good, and your confidence builds—it is as easy as that.

Exercise

Looking good. Feline good. Exercise is an important part of our well-being, and the adage of the healthy body brings the healthy mind is true. In addition, exercise is a dopamine triggering activity, as we already know. You can also draw pride from your exercise achievements, such as weight loss or completing a half-marathon, for example. The better you feel, the more confident you will become. It doesn't have to be running—you do you while cat does cat and we all go to bed happy...and wake up confident.

Have a Fearless Attitude to Life

The following quote is so good that I'm almost convinced it was said by a cat. The history books tell us that it was Mark Twain, but I'm not so sure. Either way it is very pertinent in the pursuit of living fearlessly. Join me, as we call Mark Twain a cat, and quote him as follows:

Twenty years from now you will be more disappointed by the things you didn't do than by the ones you did. So throw off the bowlines. Sail away from the safe harbor. Catch the trade winds in your sails. Explore. Dream. Discover.

This also ties in with the rocking chair–cat on lap–no regrets. The point I am making is that we shouldn't be afraid of failure. Nobody in this wide world has gone through life without succumbing to failure. Fearlesses doesn't mean stupidity, though jumping out of a plane without a parachute would be on the stupid end of the scale, and having a parachute would arguably also fall on the stupid end. Okay, bad example. Fearlessness involves making decisions with fervor, acknowledging the fact that things may not work out, but being brave in your escapades. Such an attitude will liberate you and give you a sense of freedom found inside your confidence.

Stand Up for Yourself

This is going to sound harsh, but it is so true. I must apologize in advance for the expletive, but I will beep it out in a written sense. If someone tells you that a dream or a goal of yours is unattainable, or that an idea you have had is a stupid one, you have full right to tell that person to kindly f&*k off. Believe in yourself. If you don't, nobody else will, but if you do, then others that believe in you are the important ones. Don't let negativity from others dent your aspirations. Be yourself–head up high, goals in hand, with drive and confidence.

Follow Through

If you say that you are going to do something, then make sure you go through with it. We all know someone, or we might be the someone who is always starting new things and giving them up shortly thereafter. Perhaps you want to learn to skateboard, but you try it out a few times and decide that it is too difficult. The thing is that when you take on something new, you have to be bad at it before you become good at it. You never see a baby deciding that the walking thing is too hard and giving up. Back to skating. If you start and then stop, you will grapple with the negativity of not following through, and that is bound to leave a hole in your confidence. The final sign-off on this confidence-building tip is to commit to something and stick to your commitments. You will be proud of yourself, and with pride comes confidence! Maybe you should rename your cat Confidence—your choice.

Think Long-Term

Making decisions to stay within our comfort zones in the short term can kill our confidence. Set big goals and be prepared to make sacrifices. If you want to excel academically, there will be a lot of nights that will be spent studying while your friends go out partying. Your commitment, self-discipline, and dedication are things to be proud of, and as you may have noticed, being proud has cropped up a few times so far. Pride equals confidence, and when you get that scholarship or become an intern at a company that you have always wanted to join, you will be both proud and confident. Having short-term goals is great, but throw in some medium-term and long-term goals—go old school, write them down—I know I already said that, but it bears repeating.

Do What Makes You Happy

If you are in a relationship that isn't working, get out of it. If you have a friend that always puts you down, end the friendship. Sometimes ruthlessness is required, especially when you are being mistreated by those who should have your best interests at heart. Surround yourself with the right people, and they will build your confidence and vice versa.

Self-Doubt

I realize that I have just told you to be confident, and now we are staring down the barrel at self-doubt. The reason for that is because even the most successful and most confident people in this 'crazy as a cat' world have self-doubt from time to time. It is one of the reasons that we get nervous, especially in the face of the unknown. Take a job interview, for instance. We kind of know what to expect, but not fully, so we get nervous about what might crop up. We then start doubting ourselves, even though we still display confidence. In other instances, self-doubt is a sign of low confidence, and what you are about to learn are ways to overcome self-doubt, which will also be a contributor to maintaining and improving your confidence.

Acceptance

Regarding our faults in general, if we are aware of them, then we can put measures in place to change them. The same goes for self-doubt, which could also be a result of our faults. The first thing we need to do is identify that we are harboring self-doubt, say it out loud, probably to our cats, don't judge ourselves, and make a manifesto by which we intend to control our doubt.

Have a Good Think

You need to discern whether you actually doubt yourself from only your perspective or if you are letting what others tell you, build self-doubt. This is a tough task, but we need to keep in mind that judgment from people we associate with can cause self-doubt. It is sort of like the example of people not believing in your dreams, and doubting your ability to achieve the goals you set for yourself. You have to be the driver of your confidence car, and that involves controlling self-doubt.

Shake Up the Voice Inside Your Head

Fight back and stand up to your inner voice if it continues to raise doubt and dwell on negativity. You have to accept before you change, as per the above, so you are doing no harm in acknowledging your feelings of indifference or insecurity. This shift in mindset should not be rushed, and perhaps you can use the red triangle method to clear your mind of adverse emotions and replace them with ones that promote mental wellbeing.

Admit Your Flaws

If you listen to certain people who go on about how great they are, they will start exaggerating their stories if they are not getting enough attention.

This probably points to insecurities. You know the people that I am talking about—when you say you went to Tenerife, they tell you that they have been to 'elevenerife.' That's a bit of a cheesy analogy, but it does describe the kind of person perfectly. On the subject of cheese, here is an interesting fact—mice love cheese, and cats love mice—not romantically, but in terms of eating and catching, respectively. Self-reflection helps identify your flaws, and it also leads to humility, which is a sign of contentment, as you feel no need to impress others continuously.

Be Realistic in Your Criticism

Humans are critical creatures just like cats, but we criticize ourselves, as the cats also criticize us. However, there is no need to be particularly harsh on ourselves, which would include not putting ourselves down all the time. Talk to yourself in the same way that you would talk to someone you love. You want that person to feel good about themselves, which makes you feel good about yourself, and as such can chip away at your self-doubt. Be your own biggest supporter, just not in front of your cat when she is hungry.

Appreciate Your Successes

A lot of people feel awkward getting compliments and even find it difficult to acknowledge their successes. When you succeed at work or in your personal life, it is definitely acceptable to give yourself a pat on the back. If you struggle to do so, then you can keep a success journal–basically a diary where you note your successes and can refer back to if you are having a bit of a self-doubt day (which is also acceptable).

Positivity

We hear the word often, and we know that we are meant to put positivity into action. However, we tend not to appreciate the importance of being positive and the way in which it can enrich our lives. This book is about self-improvement and personal growth, so if you want to achieve those two things, then listen up. You should have been listening from the beginning, but I guess I should say reading. Hey, read up, doesn't sound quite right. Anyway, read up or down or just read the following on eliminating negative self-talk and the impact it can have on stress reduction.

The Mechanics of Positive Thinking and Self-Talk

Contrary to popular belief, positive thinking does not mean that you ignore the hardships, worries, and problems of life. It means that your mindset towards overcoming adversity is positive, in a 'there is a solution to everything' kind of way. Ah, if only our cats experienced such things, they would teach us so much.

Self-talk is that tiny man or woman or cat inside your head that never shuts up. The man, woman, or cat can be a positive human or cute animal but can also stray towards negativity. A decent amount of inner thoughts come from logic and reason, meaning that you take a practical look at a situation. Practicality does not indicate positivity or negativity, but our inner voice does tend to fill in gaps when we have limited information. Cue the fear of the unknown. We catastrophize and think of the worst outcomes when we should be doing the opposite. When your thoughts are mainly positive, you tend to be optimistic, and the reverse is true of negative thoughts, which make you a pessimist.

Health Benefits

A study by Shonna Waters, PhD, in 2022, revealed that positivity creates a profoundly diverse set of benefits, as follows:

- Increased life span

- Lower rates of depression

- Lower levels of distress and pain

- Greater resistance to illnesses

- Better psychological and physical well-being

- Better cardiovascular health and reduced risk of death from cardiovascular disease and stroke

- Reduced risk of death from cancer

- Reduced risk of death from respiratory conditions

- Reduced risk of death from infections

- Better coping skills during hardships and times of stress

It really is quite incredible to note how powerful our brains are and how much control they exert over physical difficulties as a result of mental activity. As you can tell, positivity is definitely worth working at. When we cultivate a culture of positivity, a domino effect ensues, and our life starts to improve in various areas. There doesn't seem to be clarity on why positive thinking offers the above benefits, but there is a theory that positivity means less stress and/or better coping mechanisms which preserve the body by reducing the dangerous effects of stress.

Identifying Negative Thinking

Do our cats think negatively? It's very unlikely, and if they did, they would be able to quickly identify the negative thoughts and flip them around to the positive persuasion. It is the identifying part that is crucial. If you are driving and you see someone crossing the road up ahead, you have identified a possible danger, and thus, you slow down. If, for some reason, you fail to see the road-crosser, you will not have a need to slow down, and the results will be disastrous. Let's examine the different types of negative self-talk, so we can put ourselves in a position to identify them. We will call this step one.

Filtering

As the name suggests, you filter certain things out. This is akin to picking up on the one bad or negative thing that happened in your day and dwelling on it. The better approach, as you may have guessed, is to filter out that bad thing and focus on the positives of the day. There is an exercise called 'pit and peak.' The pit is the lowest point of your day, and the peak is the highest point. At the end of the day, write both of them down, acknowledge them, filter the pits out and immerse yourself in the positivity of the peaks.

Personalizing

Also known as the 'why me?' attitude. Bad things happen all the time, often to kind people that don't deserve them. You have got to free yourself from presuming that the world is against you. If you experience unfortunate instances or find yourself in unpleasant situations, you have to practice acceptance and address the ways to get out of or change the status quo.

Catastrophizing

I mentioned this before, but by way of a brief recap, catastrophizing is thinking the worst without knowing all the facts. Let's say a friend cancels a walk in the park that you were meant to go on together. Your immediate assumption is that it has something to do with you, and your thoughts start spiraling into a pit of negativity. The actual reason is that the person was experiencing terrible stomach cramps and could hardly even get off their couch.

Blaming Others

When something adverse befalls you, your first reaction is to push the blame onto someone else. There are times when we have to be accountable and see the situation as is before addressing the positive points about it or putting positive steps in place to improve the situation.

Should Have Could Have

Mistakes are made. We are all patently aware of that. But there is no point in dwelling on things that you should have done differently or could have implemented. Again, it is a case of acknowledging and addressing in a positive way.

Mountains and Molehills

Making a big deal about something that isn't actually as bad as you make it out to be. Things go wrong, and at the risk of repetition, you need to acknowledge and address...you know the rest–positivity and all that jazz. Jazz is actually a great name for a cat.

Perfectionism

If you allow yourself no slack and blame yourself for anything that falls short of absolute perfection, you are on a path to misery. Don't do that! I must stress that if you are a perfectionist it is not easy to get out of that mindset, but holding yourself to standards just left of impossible is not going to do you any favors.

Seeing Only Black and White

'It is either good or bad.' This isn't sound thinking...silver linings my cat-obsessed humanoids. This is also an exercise in optimism, in terms of actually seeking out the silver living in every situation.

Shifting Focus to Positive Thinking

If we are going to free ourselves from negative thinking patterns, we have to find ways of focusing on the positives. Don't worry. The search won't take long. In fact you are about to find them...lucky cats, you are.

Specify Areas That Require Change

Perhaps there are a few areas of your life that you are shrouding in negativity. You need to single them out and separate them from each other. The reason for doing so is to allow you to focus on one thought per issue that you can call on to flip the positivity switch. You want to avoid the presumption that a scenario will produce the worst possible result. When a thought like that enters your mind, you can dispel it by saying (to your cat), 'what if...' After the 'if' will come whatever it is that is the best or most positive result. You can say it out loud at home, but maybe not on the train or bus.

Check Yourself

At various times of the day, mentally assess your positivity position, and re-align your thoughts if need be. Regular checkups with the doctor, I mean the vet, are important, and so are non-negativity checks.

Don't Close Yourself Off To Humor

I'm not talking about mocking people. Only cats should get away with that. What I am saying is that you shouldn't be scared to laugh at yourself, even in difficult times. Sometimes you just need to shake your head, put a smile on your face, and say, 'this is ridiculous,' then have a chuckle. Try this one on the train or bus, and let us know how it goes.

Be Healthy

Eat well, and exercise often. Make a concerted effort to get enough sleep–No! Not one more episode before the lights go off. Turn them off now! These three healthy steps help with stress as it is, and finding the healthy body, healthy mind equilibrium is a positivity-cultivator of note.

Surround Yourself with the Right People

If you spend most of your time with negative people, it will rub off on you. Rather hang around with supportive, positive people, and you will become the same.

Affirmations

At the first identification of a negative thought, make a positive affirmation. When this starts to become routine enough that it just happens, you will be firmly on the right track.

Here are some examples of negative self-talk:

- It is too complicated for me

- I don't have the resources to complete this

task

- There is no way that it will work

- Nobody even bothers to communicate with me

- I'm never going to improve at this. I might as well just give up

And here are some examples of positive self-talk:

- I'll approach it from a different angle

- Necessity is the mother of invention (a proverb of unknown origin)

- I will try my best to make it work (note that there is no 'but' here)

- I will open the communication channels

- I'll give it a few more tries and I'm sure I will improve

Make an effort to create positivity when your negative self-talk crops up. Practice positive thinking every day. You've got this, people. I'll say it again. You've got this.

Chapter Conclusion

Right cat lovers—you have learned how to get up onto the cat walk of confidence. It all comes down to positivity and creating a good self-image. You deserve to be positive and achieve good things. Don't sell yourself short. Be the best you can be, and harvest the virtues of integrity, honesty, and kindness—to others and to yourself. Quick question before we move on. Do cats foster independence? You know the answer, and on we march.

Chapter 6

The Power of Independence

Thrive on Your Own Terms

C ats are fiercely independent. I guess I had to answer the question that I posed. Obviously, we want to be loved and we want to love others (most of us). But while doing so we also want to maintain independence. Compromise can be achieved while staying independent. In this final chapter, you will learn the secrets of self-sufficiency—secrets that our beloved cats know well. Having a support network is sometimes a necessity, but being able to operate effectively in times of solitude is equally as important. I will show you how to set healthy boundaries, nail down those passions, and do so all in the name of enjoyment...Off we prance...

Reasons to Remain Independent

As humans, we kind of suck at being independent in the first period of our life. Unlike in nature, we are pretty hopeless without our parents from birth to our teenage years, maybe a bit before. As we get older and progress through high school, we become much more independent, and we reach the point where we fly the nest when we become completely independent. It is a long road to the 'real world,' but we all take the step eventually. Being independent means more than one thing, and we need to consider independence in our careers, financially, emotionally, and in our opinions and beliefs. What follows is an analysis of the reasons for being independent, and the resultant positivity and well-being.

Independence Boosts Confidence

A sad part of life is seeing our parents grow old and lose their independence. As children, it is our responsibility to look after our parents in their old age in the same way that they looked after us until we found our independence. They will definitely be appreciative, but ultimately they don't want to have to depend on anyone. The same goes for youngsters who reach a certain age–they probably think that the age of independence is younger than it should be–no judgment. We are not all naturally independent like cats, but when we embrace our independence completely, we certainly embrace our growing confidence too.

Less Reliance on Others

It is nice when people help you out or do favors for you. If your son or daughter in another state arranges delivery of groceries or even a bunch of flowers to your house, it doesn't mean that you are reliant on them. That is why I say that we want to give love and be loved, but if we are in a situation where we do nothing and our partner does everything, it doesn't feel great. Well, it shouldn't feel great. I am, of course, not talking about human and cat relationships–they should be absolutely, positively one-sided, and you know you're not in charge. In the days when society promoted 'house-wifery,' you would often get scenarios where the husband worked all his life and the wife took care of the household. But she did not move with the times. The husband would pass away before the wife, leaving her unable to do much, especially considering how fast the world has progressed since the 1970s. That sort of blind reliance is never a good thing. So, to sum up, you just aim for one hundred percent self-reliance but enjoy the things that others do for you. You should also reciprocate.

Stress-Reduction and Happiness

This category is concerned with emotional independence, which can be challenging to achieve. That is one of the reasons why it is so difficult to leave a relationship. You are stronger than you think, and I'll be damned if you're not taking the furry guys with you. It shouldn't be up to someone else to provide you with your happiness. Often we think that if we find a partner, our lives will improve. Perhaps they will, but this thinking often results in shacking up with the wrong person, and in the end, the stress and emotional reliance are amplified. It is necessary to be emotionally independent first. Also, you don't want to drag other people into your personal decisions and emotion management. A shoulder to cry on is fine, but you should avoid constant emotional support. There are certain things that you should do on your own. I believe in you, and so do the cosmopolitan cats of the world.

Financial Independence

You would like to avoid being 30 and still living with your parents unless you have fallen on hard times. In such cases, flying back to the nest for a short time until you get onto your feet again shouldn't be a problem. Having a job and financial responsibilities that you can manage are positive points, and you should be proud of yourself. The other obvious advantage is less stress. If you know you can rely on money coming in regularly, then the peace of mind that you will have means that you can focus on other things, like self-improvement and overall well-being.

Independent Decision Making

Asking for advice is something that we all do relatively frequently, but the liberation that comes along with the ability to be an autonomous decision-maker is something to give yourself kudos for. If your decisions are influenced by others, then your independence is restricted. The four prior categories all contribute to independent decision-making. If you are not financially independent nor emotionally independent, you will always rely on others, including giving them the power to influence decision-making. If you are being financially supported by someone else, they have a certain hold over you, meaning that you are not completely free to make your own choices.

Overall Independence as a Goal

Becoming independent is a powerful motivating factor. If you want financial independence, you are motivated to get that promotion or pass the course that you are busy with so that you can get into the working world. Aiming for emotional independence can have positive effects on relationships with friends and family. Having an independent mind capable of independent thought is a wonderful asset to have. Thinking of your own volition, coming up with your own opinions, and using the information you have to make the best use of your cognition is very liberating and gives a sense of freedom.

Broader Horizons

As they say, travel broadens the mind, and although I am repeating myself, I am sure Dick Whittington's beloved cat had a mind as broad as the day is long after their infamous walk. We are not only talking about travel, but independence means freedom—freedom to meet new people. Freedom to do new things. Freedom to enjoy your independence in the ways that you want to.

Independence widens the world in one sense but narrows it in another. It breeds opportunity and puts you in a place where you can achieve great things.

The Importance of Self-Value

Being independent can result in holding yourself in a higher regard. You are bringing value to society in general, as well as adding value to your relationships. When you become independent in every way discussed, your sense of self-worth improves. With increased self-worth comes increased chances of personal success. That is the end goal.

Nietzsche

You may have heard of the 19th-century philosopher Friedrich Nietzsche. If not, that's okay (he's not the one who said, 'I think, therefore I am.' That was Descartes). In any event, I think it is appropriate to end this section with a Nietzsche quote. It is in old weirdo English, but it is just so appropriate in its address of independence. Here we go:

It is the business of the very few to be independent; it is a privilege of the strong. And whoever attempts it, even with the best right, but without being OBLIGED to do so, proves that he is probably not only strong, but also daring beyond measure. He enters into a labyrinth, he multiplies a thousandfold the dangers which life in itself already brings with it; not the least of which is that no one can see how and where he loses his way, becomes isolated, and is torn piecemeal by some minotaur of conscience. Supposing such a one comes to grief, it is so far from the comprehension of men that they neither feel it, nor sympathize with it. And he cannot any longer go back! He cannot even go back again to the sympathy of men (Brown, 2013).

You have to agree that our man, 'Niech,' said it well. He must have loved cats.

The Sweet Silence of Solitude

A lot of us have watched enough prison shows or documentaries to know that solitary confinement has no benefits whatsoever. But we are not talking about such extremes. Some of us like having company all the time. However, there are many people who find it exhausting and need to spend time alone to recharge. Then you get those individuals who just prefer their own company. I guess you could call them loners, and if they are happy living a life of solitude, then we have no right to question it.

In the last decade, there have been an increasing number of studies into solitude. One such study, published on the Sage Journals website, was concerned with potential changes in human emotions after being in a solitary setting. The study distinguished between high arousal and low arousal emotions. The former would be energization and excitement, and the latter would be calmness and relaxation. Both high and low arousal emotion types in these instances are positive. However, high and low arousal emotions on a negative scale were also categorized. They would be anger and anxiety on the high arousal side and loneliness and sadness on the low arousal side.

Among other findings, it was concluded that 'time spent alone offers a unique opportunity for arousal regulation' (Nguyen, et al., 2017). In simple terms, high arousal emotions, whether positive or negative, drop to a lower state of arousal during alone time. Scientists have labeled this the 'deactivation effect' (Nguyen, et al., 2017).

I don't know if we can say that the results were predictable, but the conclusion was that people who enjoy and embrace solitude experience an increase in calm and relaxation. People who do not enjoy solitude experience increased sadness and loneliness. It makes you wonder if a study was really necessary–I could have come to that conclusion. Okay, sorry science, I know you will look into anything possible.

Anyway, there is still a widespread belief that time alone should be used for self-reflection and that if done correctly, it can heal the soul. If you think about it, solitude isn't just sitting on your own, not doing anything. Solitude may involve fly fishing or a long walk. It is safe to say that solitude is not for everyone, but it is still necessary to explore it a bit more. Positive self-reflection when in a silent and peaceful environment is good for you. Of that, I have no doubt. All the things we discussed earlier about recognizing negativity, mistakes, bad decisions, and the like are exercises that can be done in solitude. But we have to be careful to avoid personal judgment and to learn from the experiences or come up with positive spins. I have no problem with that. However, when in solitude, many of us tend to worry and let regrets ruminate in our minds. My advice is to try out a bit of solitary self-reflection, and if you feel sad, lonely, or anxious, then turn your back on solitude. If it is not completely unbearable, you can look at putting some mindfulness exercises into practice. However, if mindfulness works better for you at home in a comfortable chair, then you have my blessing and the collective blessings of the cat population.

Boundaries

Independence requires boundaries and boundary setting can be tricky. We have boundaries at work, with friends, in relationships, and with ourselves. The great thing with boundaries is that when they are set, all parties involved know what they can and can't do. We can look at boundaries like different rule books applicable independently to different situations. There are friendships where the boundaries are not clearly set and one person takes advantage of the other because of it. Let's begin with that.

Boundaries in Friendships

Something that I have witnessed several times in friendships is one person exploiting the other financially. It can happen in small ways. Here is an example. You have a friend that you visit regularly, and often she will invite you over for a coffee. Just before you are ready to leave home, she sends you a text asking you to pick up a box of cigarettes for her on your way. In the text, she says that she will pay you back when you arrive. Being a friend, you acquiesce and grab the cigarettes on the way to her house. She thanks you for the cigarettes and tells you that she doesn't have any cash on her but that she will give you the money the next time she sees you. Like many of us, you feel awkward asking, and she doesn't say anything when you meet up again. The same pattern repeats, and you never get your money. The longer you leave it, the greater the issue becomes in your mind, and it reaches a point where you start feeling resentment. Situations like this are unhealthy and don't do a lot of good for your mental well-being.

You are partially to blame, but a friend should never put you in that position. First off, it is such a strange human trait that we feel awkward to ask for money that is owed to us. That isn't quite the point, but interesting nonetheless. Had you set a boundary after the first time it happened, you could have avoided being taken advantage of. Right at the outset, you could have said to your friend that you would buy her a pack this time but that you won't do so in the future because you have been in similar situations and have been out of pocket. There is nothing wrong with taking that approach, and once the boundary is set, then both parties have clarity, know where they stand, and a resentment situation is off the cards. The same would apply with friends asking to borrow money. If you say no the first time you are asked, then the boundary is set, and the other person should respect you enough to respect the boundary, and not ask again.

Another example would be affection. There are many people who are not fond of physical touch. Some prefer to shake hands, others like a hug, and some enjoy a hug and a kiss as a greeting. If you are a hugger, but a friend of yours feels uncomfortable in hugging situations, you could go for a high five or fist bump, as long as there is clarity from the outset. Just like the cigarette example, the boundary must be established early on. The rules are set, and everyone involved knows not to break them. Such is the breeding ground for healthy relationships.

Family should generally trump friendships. If you are spending time with a friend and you get a call from your husband or wife to tell you that your child is ill or is having an issue with something, you should leave to attend to the family matter. Any good parent would do the same, and if your friends know from the outset that you love them but that family will always come first, then a healthy boundary is in place. Again, it is about clarity in the beginning, which leads to ongoing clarity.

Boundaries in Romantic Relationships

We are aware that communication is the key to a successful relationship—well, one of the keys. They can be complicated in terms of expectations from either side. When a couple is still getting to know each other, there are things about their past, perhaps, that they are not comfortable discussing in the early stages. Establishing that certain topics are off the table for the moment is a smart implementation of a boundary. Someone will speak about something when they are ready. There should also be physical boundaries so both parties are aware that one or both of them are not ready for physical intimacy. Another case of the rule book being written and then respected.

Boundaries at Work

We spend a significant period of our lives working, and our jobs often involve being thrust together with people that we ordinarily wouldn't be friends with. That is why there are clashes, disagreements, office politics, and *crossing* of boundaries. Not always, but it does happen often. We can divide work boundaries into some categories that can help us to effectively create the rules.

Saying No

This is important in an effort to avoid being taken advantage of. You can refer back to the 'No. Yes. No.' concept. Having work delegated to you is fine, but when time does not allow you to give it your best effort, you need to say no but make a suggestion as to another option. Being asked to do something that goes against your principles is encouraged. As long as everyone in the work environment is aware, then a healthy situation is propagated.

Structure

Different people structure their days in different ways. If you need an hour or two where you are not disturbed, then set such a rule early on. At the end of the day, it will benefit all concerned. Logically, your 'don't disturb' time is advantageous to the company because you will get more done. There should be respect from bosses and colleagues alike, allowing you what you have requested.

Caution Towards Communication

We should avoid getting involved in gossip sessions and office politics. You need to make your co-workers aware that you are not prepared to engage in such things. Eradicate early, and pat yourself on the back for doing so. In work environments, you do get people who will try to push their own ideologies or beliefs onto you. Doing so can be a serious boundary breaker, which is also something to be aware of and to make part of the rule book.

Setting Other General Boundaries

If you are not comfortable discussing politics or religion, for instance, then make that part of your boundary rule book. Of course, you don't want to come across as brash or militant. These conversations and rule-noting exercises should be done politely and respectfully.

Purrrrsue Your Passions and Enjoy the Journey

We have talked about patience, but I had to use the play on the word 'pursue' tactic, as above. So, on that note, you know from the sections on finding your passions that doing so will be fulfilling and, furthermore, will help with your personal growth. So be like a sleek, silent cat stalking its prey with no intention of giving up.

On the enjoyment point, self-improvement should not be seen as a destination but a journey. It is ongoing, and when you achieve your well-being goals, you should be proud of yourself. Don't look at exercises like mindfulness from an ultra-serious perspective. It is easy to forget to practice acute focus, and if you have a rushed morning full of stress like the one we discussed earlier, forgive yourself for it. Rejoice in the times that you wake up a bit earlier and enjoy all the facets of the readiness process. As you get better, you will establish better routines, and once you get into those routines, all aspects of life start improving.

Chapter Conclusion

Independence is something that we should all strive for. Perhaps we should take it like a journey from childhood, where our independence is zero, through to our current position. Wherever we are currently placed in life in terms of independence will differ, but it is also something ongoing. Life has its ups and downs, but we need to aim for the liberation that comes with being independent financially, emotionally, and in any other area. Basically, aiming for autonomy of independence as a goal and the maintenance of independence as the long game.

Solitude is not independence, don't get that wrong. It works for some of us and is disastrous for others. Try it out and do some self-reflection. If it isn't your bag, then you don't have to carry it on. I am not going to mention the science again because it is more of an individual than an empirical thing.

Then there are the boundaries that we need to set as early as possible in the different situations discussed above. The earlier you write the rule book, the better the understanding by all parties. Stalk your passions just like your cat stalks its prey, and see the journey to self-improvement and personal health as one that is ongoing. Lastly, have fun and enjoy the process, in the knowledge that you are constantly improving yourself and experiencing life in the best way possible–like a cat–you lucky thing.

Conclusion

Well, all you cat lovers and self-improvement seekers out there, we have reached the end of the stalk to freedom. Congratulations on your focus and attention, and well done for implementing what we have learned. If you have not started implementing, I encourage you to do so, and you will revel in the results.

Cats have taught us a lot, and they will continue to do so. They are complicated in one sense, and simple in another. The same could be said for us humans, even though our cats know that we are inferior in every sense...only just. Every person has the power to take control of their life, and I would venture to say that after having read this book, you would agree with me.

With the right 'cattitude,' you can put the tips and advice, exercises, and suggestions in motion. You know what they are, and this conclusion will act as a summary of the most important and pertinent sections. The idea is for you to have a concise point of reference that will jog your memory and allow you to return to the concepts that you would like to revisit. I hope that every section has struck a chord and that the message has been clearly delivered. I am confident that it has been well received, so let's get to the summary of what you have learned.

Being unique is a good thing, and you need to embrace your uniqueness by telling yourself that it's a good thing. Your life is your story, and your diversity is what keeps the pages turning. You have fears, just like everyone else, and we all need to face them at some stage. Be the buffalo, not the cow, and don't forget to feed the meow machine.

You know by now that you can't please everyone, but you must focus on pleasing yourself. In order to do so you need to practice self-acceptance and self-love. Like-minded people will help you with that, and when you receive criticism, be comfortable with it and make a change if you need to. Self-accountability is a necessity (while we are talking double barrel words starting with 'self').

If you are uncomfortable with your talents or you haven't uncovered them yet, then a self-assessment test is an excellent idea. In addition to the test you can pinpoint your talents by identifying what makes you feel good, where you spend your money, and based on opinions of loved ones. Praise that you receive can also inform you of your talents, but you should still be open to change if required.

Turn your talents into passions, or explore other areas of life that you could be passionate about. Remember the six vital human needs? Certainty, significance, variety, growth, and contribution. Explore them all, feel fulfilled and practice the rocking chair test to identify the things you should be doing now.

Rest and relaxation are needed to reset and re-align with self-growth. Our cats are amazing at it, and you can take lessons from them. Focus on your breathing, be creative, and allow yourself the freedom to day dream. Don't worry, you will land on your feet. Mindfulness is your ally and you are now aware of how deep focus on the mundane can be a fantastic distraction, as is the case with the mindful meditation body scan. Tricky at first, but don't forget about the red triangle to bring you back.

Be curious like your kittens and 'catties.' It will lead you to new experiences, which will provide fulfillment and allow appreciation. Curiosity places us outside our comfort zones, which keeps us on our feet (toes). The possibilities of finding your purpose, making memories, and experiencing life are all real thanks to your curiosity. Plus, it is healthy for your brain and builds your humble side. Take a walk, explore, and reflect, among the other tips provided. Do a puzzle, volunteer to help in some way, or involve yourself in different hobbies or interests.

Growing as a person and finding fulfillment involves communication, which comes in various forms. You know how to get along in small talk situations, and also how important body language is. The important lessons from the section on body language were looking people in the eye, offering a firm handshake, and smiling, among other positives. On the negative side, you shouldn't fidget, frown, or make too much eye contact—awkwardness can be the result.

On the talking front, you know that you need to hear, but also listen. Practicing empathy is a vital skill within the auspices of listening, which should be accompanied by patience. To engage in meaningful conversations that form human connection, we need to trust and show that we are worthy of trust. This doesn't mean that you always have to say yes to everyone all the time. The ability to say no is important, so remember the 'yes, no, yes' exercise. In addition, know what your conversation exit lines are, and leave without fidgeting or looking flustered. Bring the conversation full circle and exit gracefully, using the tips in chapter four.

Confidence is something that is often not natural, but as you now know there are ways to build confidence and ways to improve confidence. When you get things done and can tick them off a list, you feel a sense of achievement, and that builds confidence. Doing the right thing when nobody's watching should create pride in yourself and hence up your confidence levels. Exercise releases the dopamine that picks you up and approaching life fearlessly also cranks up the confidence. You have to stand up for yourself and when you say you are going to do something, following through is a must.

Every single one of us experiences self-doubt, so don't expect it never to crop up, but rather know what to do when it does. You know how to accept and acknowledge self-doubt, then have a think about it, and retrain your inner voice. Your cat has flaws and so do you. Wait, only you have flaws, but so do all the other humans. Admit them, don't be overly critical, but definitely do enjoy and appreciate your successes, big and small.

Be positive through thinking patterns and self-talk. You are aware that humans are negative beings, not like cats, who can't really be bothered–in the best and cutest way possible. Keep in mind that positive thinking means health benefits, and use that notion to identify negative thoughts, and flip them around.

The idea is to filter out the negative by getting rid of catastrophizing and personalizing everything as a self-blame exercise. Don't dwell on what could have happened, and leave the molehills as molehills, never to become mountains. If you need to change, then change! Be open to humor, hang around with the people that are right for you, and keep your affirmations going strong.

If you can be as independent as your cat then you are in the driver's seat of your self-improvement vehicle. Independence in a financial, emotional, and overall sense are big assets, and not having to rely on anyone is the end goal...except kitten cat, you can rely on her.

Try out solitude. If you love it, carry it on. If you hate it, don't go back.

Finally, be good at setting boundaries in your friendships, relationships, and at work. Then, a final reminder to purrrrrsue your passions (with an extra 'r' for effect).

There we have it, you are well on your way to self-improvement and I know that you are growing every day. So, feed the cat, put your feet up, anticipate the cantankerous disposition to come, along with snuggles, nuzzles, and back arching. Then, feel free to leave a review of this book, and accept my gratitude that you have made it this far.

As a final send off, I would like to leave you with a quote:

"I am standing on your face because it is time to wake up and feed me" (every cat since the beginning of time).

Your feedback matters! Scan the QR code above to share your thoughts on Amazon. Thank you for joining this amazing journey!

A Free Gift to The Readers

Thank you for choosing to read this book. I hope you find it insightful and practical.

To enhance your experience and provide additional value, I've included the following material at no extra cost to you:

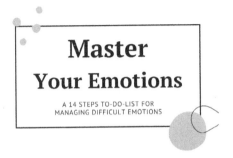

This supplementary content offers valuable insights related to managing your emotions.

To access your bonus material, please scan the QR code below:

Thank you for your support, and enjoy your reading!

References

(2019). 10 Ways to Improve Your Curiosity. https://curiosity.britannica.com/10-ways-to-improve-your-curiosity

(2021). Relaxation: Tips and Exercises to Help You Relax. https://www.mind.org.uk/information-support/tips-for-everyday-living/relaxation/relaxation-tips/#.XL CEAjBKipo

(2022, February 3). Stress Management. https://www.mayoclinic.org/healthy-lifestyle/stress-management/in-depth/positive-thinking/art-20043 950

Cognitive Behavioral Therapy. https://www.mayoclinic.org/tests-procedures/cognitive-behavioral-therapy/about/pac-20384610

Getting Started with Mindfulness. https://www.mindful.org/meditation/mindfulness-getting-started

Top 10 Facts About Smiling. https://www.funkidslive.com/learn/top-10-facts/top-10-facts-about-smiling

Why is Conversation Important?
https://www.conversationagent.com/2015/10/why-conversation-matters

Bridges, F. (2017, July 21). 10 Ways to Build Confidence. https://www.forbes.com/sites/francesbridges/2017/07/21/10-ways-to-build-confidence/?sh=34ec90c23c59

Brook, J. (2022, November 25). 10 Hobbies to Build Confidence and Self-Esteem in Yourself. https://everydaypower.com/10-hobbies-build-confidence-self-esteem

Brown, J. (2013, June 17). 8 Important Reasons Why You Should be More Independent. https://addicted2success.com/life/8-important-reasons-why-you-should-be-more-independent

Donovan, P. (2002, December 16). Study Finds that Curiosity Is Key to Personal Growth in Many Spheres, Including Intimate Relationships. https://www.buffalo.edu/news/releases/2002/12/5996

Gunel, S. (202, February 4). How to Overcome Self-Doubt and Build Confidence. https://medium.com/swlh/how-to-overcome-self-doubt-and-build-confidence-41d9639efd85

Hill, J. (2021, April 2). 14 Reasons to Always Try New Things. https://www.lifehack.org/902478/try-new-things

Kholghi, B. (2023). 13 Ways to Embrace Your Uniqueness in 2023. https://www.coaching-online.org/your-uniqueness

Lenhardt, (2019, August 21). 97 Interesting Body Language Facts. https://www.factretriever.com/body-language-facts

Nguyen, T. (2017, October 26). Solitude as an Approach to Effective Self-Regulation. https://journals.sagepub.com/doi/10.1177/01461672177 33073

Nguyen, T. (2023, February 13). The Power of Solitude. https://thebeautifultruth.org/life/the-power-of-solit ude

Raymond, H. (2016). The Art of Nonverbal Communication in Practice. https://journals.lww.com/thehearingjournal/fulltext /2016/05000/the_art_of_nonverbal_communicatio n_in_practice.5

Robbins, T. (2023). 10 Ways to Find Your Passion in Life. https://www.tonyrobbins.com/personal-growth/ho w-to-find-passion

Romano, C. (2023, April 3). 13 Ways to Identify Your Talents and Utilize Them. https://www.lifehack.org/articles/productivity/10-w ays-identify-your-talents-and-utilize-them

Seleg, M. (2017, April 18). How Do Work Breaks Help Your Brain? 5 Surprising Answers.
https://www.psychologytoday.com/ca/blog/change power/201704/how-do-work-breaks-help-your-brai n-5-surprising-answers

Waters, S. (2022, April 12). Improve Your Life with a New Outlook: 10 Benefits of Positive Thinking.
https://www.betterup.com/blog/positive-thinking-b enefits